THE RANDOM WALK GUIDE TO INVESTING

THE RANDOM WALK GUIDE TO INVESTING

Ten Rules for Financial Success

Burton G. Malkiel

Viva Books

New Delhi | Mumbai | Chennai | Kolkata | Bengaluru | Hyderabad | Kochi | Guwahati

First Indian Edition 2011

VIVA BOOKS PRIVATE LIMITED

- 4737/23 Ansari Road, Daryaganj, New Delhi 110 002
  E-mail: vivadelhi@vivagroupindia.net, Tel. 42242200
- 76, Service Industries, Shirvane, Sector 1, Nerul, Navi Mumbai 400 706
  E-mail: vivamumbai@vivagroupindia.net, Tel. 27721273, 27721274
- Jamals Fazal Chambers, 26 Greams Road, Chennai 600 006
  E-mail: vivachennai@vivagroupindia.net, Tel. 28290304, 28294241
- B-103, Jindal Towers, 21/1A/3 Darga Road, Kolkata 700 017
  E-mail: vivakolkata@vivagroupindia.net, Tel. 22836381, 22816713
- 7, Sovereign Park Apartments, 56-58, K. R. Road, Basavanagudi, Bengaluru 560 004
  E-mail: vivabangalore@vivagroupindia.net, Tel. 26607409, 26607410
- 101-102 Mughal Marc Apartments, 3-4-637 to 641, Narayanguda, Hyderabad 500 0
  E-mail: vivahyderabad@vivagroupindia.net, Tel. 27564481, 27564482
- Beevi Towers, First Floor, SRM Road, Kaloor, Kochi 682 018, Kerala
  E-mail: vivakochi@vivagroupindia.net, Tel: 0484-2403055, 2403056
- 232, GNB Road, Beside UCO Bank, Silpukhuri, Guwahati 781 003
  E-mail: vivaguwahati@vivagroupindia.net, Tel: 0361-2666386

www.vivagroupindia.com

Published by arrangement with
W. W. Norton & Company, Inc.
500 Fifth Avenue
New York NY 10110

This edition is for sale in the Indian subcontinent only. Not for export elsewhere.

ISBN : 978-81-309-1590-6

Published by Vinod Vasishtha for Viva Books Private Limited, 4737/23, Ansari Road, Daryaganj, New Delhi-110 002.

Printed and bound by Mehta Offset Private Limited, New Delhi.

FOR

Farfie & Skippy Doo

CONTENTS

Preface and Acknowledgments *xvii*

PART ONE: THE BASICS 1

BASIC POINT 1:
FIRE YOUR INVESTMENT ADVISER 5

BASIC POINT 2:
FOCUS ON FOUR INVESTMENT CATEGORIES 11

Cash 12

Bonds 13

Common Stocks 15

Bubbles in Stock Prices • The Tulip-Bulb Craze
The South Sea Bubble • The Internet Craze
What Lessons Should We Learn?

Real Estate 24

BASIC POINT 3:
UNDERSTAND THE RISK/RETURN RELATIONSHIP 27

PART TWO: THE RULES 33

RULE 1:
START SAVING NOW, NOT LATER:
TIME IS MONEY 37

Returns Throughout U.S. History 38

The Miracle of Compound Interest 38

The Million-Dollar Difference 40

RULE 2:
KEEP A STEADY COURSE:
THE ONLY SURE ROAD TO WEALTH
IS REGULAR SAVINGS 42

Savvy Savings Tips 43

1. Pay Yourself First

2. Find a Save More Tomorrow Plan

3. Make Out a Budget

4. Change a Spending Habit or Two

5. Think in Terms of Opportunity Costs

6. Be Saving in Your Spending

7. Pay Off Your Credit Card Balance

Strategies for Catching Up 50

1. Downsize Your Lifestyle and Start Saving Now

2. Consider Pushing Retirement Back a Few Years

3. Make the Most of Your Home Equity

Retirement Planning 52

The Millionaire Next Door 54

RULE 3:

DON'T BE CAUGHT EMPTY-HANDED:
INSURANCE AND CASH RESERVES 57

Establishing a Cash Reserve 57

Money-Market Mutual Funds 58

Bank Certificates of Deposit (CDs) 60

Internet Banks 61

Treasury Bills 61

Tax-Exempt Money-Market Funds 62

Buying Insurance 63

Variable Annuities 67

RULE 4:

STIFF THE TAX COLLECTOR 68

Individual Retirement Accounts 69

Roth IRAs 71

Pension Plans 73

401(k) and 403(b) Pension Plans • Self-Employed Plans
What Can You Invest In?

Priorities in Saving for Retirement 75

A Caveat 77

Possible New Tax-Favored Vehicles 77

Tax-Free Savings Strategies for Education 78

Saving for College: As Easy as 529
Education Savings Accounts • Education Savings Bonds

The Best Tax Strategy of All 81

RULE 5:
MATCH YOUR ASSET MIX TO YOUR INVESTMENT PERSONALITY: HOW TO ALLOCATE YOUR ASSETS 83
A Reminder: Risk and Return Again 84
Your Time Horizon 87
Your Capacity for Risk 90
Your Temperament 92
Rebalancing, or Keeping an Even Temperament 94

RULE 6:
NEVER FORGET THAT DIVERSITY REDUCES ADVERSITY 96
The Benefits of Diversification 96
An Investment Horror Story 98
The Potential Crises in Some 401(k) Plans 99
How Much Diversification Is Enough? 100
Do You Need to Diversify Internationally? 103
Diversification Also Means Buying Other Asset Classes 104
Diversification Over Time 106

RULE 7:
PAY YOURSELF, NOT THE PIPER 111
Pay Off All Credit Card Bills 112
Look Out for Mutual Fund Expenses 113

Costs Matter for All Financial Products 115

Don't Get Wrapped Up 117

RULE 8:

BOW TO THE WISDOM OF THE MARKET 118

Why the Market Is Smarter Than You Are 119

Being Smarter Doesn't Always Mean Being Smart 122

Timing Isn't Everything 122

Why Do Most Professionals Get C's? 124

But Don't Some Active Managers Beat the Market Every Year? 127

Managers Who Deserve an A 131

1. The Role of Chance

2. They Did It Their Way

3. You Never Know in Advance Who the Winners Will Be

RULE 9:

BACK PROVEN WINNERS: MODEL PORTFOLIOS OF INDEX FUNDS 135

The Index Advantage 136

But Not All Index Funds Are Alike 138

Exchange Traded Funds 139

Indexing Works for Bonds, Real Estate, and Other Asset Classes 141

What Index and What Funds Should Be Chosen? 142

A Life-Cycle Guide to Asset Allocation 146

RULE 10:
DON'T BE YOUR OWN WORST ENEMY:
AVOID STUPID INVESTOR TRICKS 153

Overconfidence 154

Herding 156

Illusion of Control 160

Loss Aversion 162

Other Psychological Pitfalls 163

Susceptibility to Hot Tip Investing

Gin Rummy Behavior • Believing in Foolproof Schemes

Ignoring Costs 165

Getting Entranced by New Issues 166

PART THREE: TAKING STOCK

AN INVESTMENT SCORECARD 169

Questions Frequently Asked About Indexing 176

A Summing Up 181

REFERENCES 185

INDEX 189

The

RANDOM WALK GUIDE TO INVESTING

Preface and Acknowledgments

ACADEMICS LOVE to communicate. Some even like to practice what they preach. I do my practicing by sitting on the investment committees for some large institutional investors controlling hundreds of billions of dollars of assets. My preaching, I found, was too often restricted to my peers. I think it is important and useful for academics also to write for a broader audience, particularly on subjects of interest to the general public. This helps shorten the lag between academic discovery and practical application. I have so thoroughly enjoyed my own forays into this arena that I have been persuaded to do so again.

In 1973, I wrote *A Random Walk Down Wall Street,* which was largely devoted to an exposition of academic research on the stock market. The book has been highly successful and it is now in its eighth edition. But the book is 500 pages long and filled with tables and charts. Many folks who need financial advice may not be willing to invest the time reading it. For that reason, Drake McFeely, my publisher, one day asked me an intriguing question: "Do you think you could write a book of less than 200 pages in length that boils down the time-tested advice from *Random Walk* into an investment guide that would be completely accessible for a reader who knows nothing about the securities markets and who hates numbers?"

As a serial communicator, I was immediately taken with the idea. The more I have studied securities markets and gained practical experience in investment management, the more I am convinced that there is a very simple step-by-step strategy that will allow individual investors to obtain better returns with less risk than even the sophisticated professionals achieve. The result is this book designed to be comprehensive and practical—easily readable and completely accessible even to the lay reader. It is truly the only investment guide you need.

My debts of gratitude to people who have assisted me are enormous. A number of research assistants have provided invaluable help. These include Tim Kirby, Derek Jun, Ananya Lodaya, Adam Rilander, Ray Wang, and Basak Yeltekin. Especially, helpful analyses were completed by Costin Bontas. Much of the data used in showing how my recommendations have withstood the test of time were provided by the Vanguard Group of Investment Companies. Kevin Loughlin and Crystal Shannon were very helpful in gathering data and Ker Moua was indispensable in quickly responding to what must have seemed like hundreds of data requests.

I have been extremely fortunate to have the services of my assistant, Diana Prout, during the preparation of this book. She miraculously transcribed my scribble or dictation into readable text. I also benefited from the typing assistance of Phyllis Fafalios and Karen Neukirchen.

A vital contribution was made by Patricia Taylor, a professional writer and editor, who has helped me with several projects in the past. She read through the entire manuscript and made numerable contributions to the style, organization, and content of the manuscript. Pat has an uncanny ability to read a draft I have written and find the questions that I had failed to address but that are sure to be on the minds of the lay reader.

My association with W. W. Norton continues to be a very pleasant one. Drake McFeely served as my editor and his suggestions were particularly helpful in pushing me to present the "Investment Scorecard" and "Frequently Asked Questions" in the third part of the book. His assistant, Eve Lazovitz, also helped in many ways, as did Ann Adelman, the manuscript editor.

As in everything I do, my wife, Nancy, made the most essential contribution. She read through two drafts of this manuscript and improved the exposition immeasurably. More important, no one could give an author more love and support. And no one could be a greater source of joy—not even Skippy Doo.

Part One

THE BASICS

Albert Einstein was one of the true geniuses of the twentieth century. When considering the complexity of various models of the physical sciences, he remarked, "Everything should be made as simple as possible." What's good enough for Einstein is good enough for me—and should be for you, too, particularly when it comes to the world of investing. The rules for achieving financial security through savings and investment are extraordinarily simple. They may require a small degree of self-sacrifice. They do involve discipline and stick-to-itiveness. But obtaining well above average investment results is strikingly easy, and this book will tell you how to do it.

I realize that the investment world often appears to be frighteningly complex. It features terms like "shorts," "puts," and "straddles," and it involves financial instruments—such as TIPS, ETFs, and HOLDRS—that appear to have been taken from an eye chart. The market offers a bewildering array of investment opportunities. It's even possible now to buy and sell the rights to emit carbon dioxide—yes, you can actually make money trading smog.

Don't be befuddled by the jargon and the seemingly incomprehensible financial offerings. Just remember that beneath all the rhetoric and the gimmicks lie some very simple rules. That's what this book is all about. It tells you everything you need to know to achieve financial security through savings and investment. By following the rules presented here, you will be able to achieve investment results that will put the pros to shame. Before you start, however, you need to take three crucial steps. These are described in Part One.

BASIC POINT ONE

Fire Your Investment Adviser

THE SAD TRUTH is that there are only three kinds of financial prognosticators: those who don't know, those who don't know they don't know, and those who know they don't know but who get paid big bucks to pretend they know. What are they good for? Their primary interest is not yours, but theirs: they are very good at making money for themselves.

Fred Schwed, Jr., in his charming and witty exposé of the financial community in the 1930s, tells the story of an investor's first visit to lower Manhattan. The investor was shown large numbers of expensive yachts that were moored close to Wall Street and was told that these were the yachts of the most successful brokers. The investor asked, "Where are the customers' yachts?" Today, the most successful professionals in the financial community are more likely to have Gulfstreams rather than yachts, but the principle is the same. These folks are looking out for their own well-being—not yours.

Financial advisers are generally compensated by earning commissions on the products they sell you. Thus, they have a vested interest in making the investment process seem as complicated as possible so that you must turn to them for advice. And they are likely to push those products on which they make the largest commission—not those that are likely to line your pockets. Financial service companies want you to believe that you can't make financial decisions yourself so that they can collect lucrative fees. Remember the words of Woody Allen: "A stockbroker is someone who invests other people's money until it is all gone."

Jane Bryant Quinn, author of *Making the Most of Your Money*, quotes from a letter she received from a stockbroker, which describes the situation with uncharacteristic honesty:

> *The first thing a securities salesman learns is to gain the confidence of his customer. This enables the salesman to more easily sell the customer the products that pay the salesman the highest commission. All securities firms have different commission schedules for different investment products. Most firms will respond that their brokers are free to sell their customers any investment product they wish. But in practice, the broker-salesman is "encouraged" to sell the product most profitable to the firm and do it often. All securities firms also have formulas that indicate how often customers' money should turn over, and these are considered minimums. . . .*
>
> *I, too, have fallen prey to the siren's song of wealth and glamour that has been and is Wall Street. I have overtraded customer accounts, and bought for them "investments" that made more sense for me than them. I guess I wrote [to you] as*

a catharsis, and to clear my head and that of my colleagues of the siren's song.

Signed Anonymous

While everyone recognizes that brokers make their living by charging commissions, Wall Street still manages to conceal one very nasty secret: The financial "experts" know precious little more than you know. In fact, I will go out on a limb and tell you that the experts have no idea what stocks you should buy to provide superior future returns. A blindfolded chimpanzee throwing darts at the stock pages can select individual stocks as well as the experts. We will see later that the correct investment strategy is actually to throw a towel over the stock pages and buy a low-cost mutual fund that includes all stocks and does no trading. The sum total value of all the financial data, commentary, opinion, and advice you hear from the media or your financial professional is less than zero. In fact, the "buy" recommendations of Wall Street firms (especially those that tout the stocks of their banking clients) do no better than the few stocks they tell you to "sell." And a good way to go broke quickly is to purchase stock issues (initial public offerings) immediately after they start trading.

Pay no heed to the financial professionals who declare that they know what the stock market will do and what stocks or mutual funds you should buy. Cover stories on the "hottest" stock or "the best" mutual fund for the period ahead may help to sell the investment magazines, but the recommendations are worthless.

And tune out the financial TV channels that feature investment "experts" who make breathless forecasts of the stocks that are poised to double. Pay no heed to the gurus who offer heavily jargoned clichés about the day's market activity. What can you possibly learn from platitudes that pass for insights, such as "Today's decline was caused by buyers moving to the sidelines awaiting a clearer definition of the trend." How many times have you heard an "expert" tell you that "the market rose today because there were more buyers than sellers." Of course, for a trade to happen at all there must be both a buyer and a seller. Money honeys may be pleasing to the eye but not to your pocketbook. You can't blame the TV producers for trying to make it interesting. After all, their job is to produce as many eyeballs as possible for advertisers so that you won't switch channels to watch Stone Cold Steve Austin body-slam the Rock. As they say on the wrestling shows, "Don't try this at home." Following the advice of these financial "experts" can be hazardous to your wealth. One writer, Nassim Nicholas Taleb, author of *Fooled by Randomness*, suggests that you listen to CNBC with the sound off so that the facial expressions and body gyrations of the "experts" seem humorous and you'll be less likely to follow their advice.

It is incomprehensible to me that consumers will spend hours researching the merits of various $50 portable CD players yet will casually spend thousands of dollars to buy a stock that has been hyped in a TV interview, a brokerage report, or even worse on a rumor or stock tip from one's golfing buddy or brother-in-law. Investors are incredibly credulous. Professional market strategists and analysts make predictions and recommend trades because trades generate revenues for their employers—not because they really have any expert knowledge that no one else possesses. Cancel your subscriptions to worthless investment magazines and newsletters. At least 95 percent of what you will read or hear will be worthless. Watch the cooking channel or the gardening channel if you want useful advice. Heed the advice of comedian Lily Tomlin: "No matter how cynical you become, it's never enough to keep up."

In the early 2000s, *Forbes* magazine editorialized:

> During the last year as well as for the year before—but heck, let's just say for the whole screaming decade that's now in the grave—your average pro on Wall Street has failed to beat the indexes. . . . No, your average Wall Street pro hasn't beaten a dart tossed by a drunk in a bus depot since 1994. . . . For five years running the pros have had their jockstraps yanked up to their earlobes by the Beardstown Ladies.

In fact, *Forbes* would later learn that these folksy midwestern ladies who claimed to have achieved phenomenal investment results and who interlaced their stock-market advice with recipes such as "stock market muffins guaranteed to rise" were, in fact, cooking the books as well. Their published returns had been wildly inflated by counting their club dues as investment returns.

Even in fields such as medicine where true expertise really does exist, the greatest gains come from following simple advice. Despite all the gains from various wonder drugs, gene therapy, and new surgical techniques, Charles Ellis, author of *The Loser's Game*, reminds us that most medical progress has come from one old invention and one simple technique. More lives have been saved and prolonged by penicillin and by washing hands than by any other pharmaceutical or medical technique.

As Malcolm Forbes realized a long time ago, the way to get rich from investment advice is to sell it—not to take it.

Charles Ellis points out, "It must be apparent to intelligent investors that if anyone possessed the ability [to forecast stock prices] consistently and accurately, he would become a billionaire so quickly that he would not find it necessary to sell his stock market guesses to the general public." Tune out the TV investment gurus who dispense worthless advice. I promise you that the simple rules given here are all the investment advice you will ever need. Moreover, by keeping your savings and investment strategy as simple as possible, you will free up the time to do the really important things you want to do in your life such as spending more time with friends and family.

Once you've fired your financial adviser and canceled the subscriptions to all your investment magazines, you may be pleasantly surprised that you now have quite a few extra dollars to invest. Don't rush into doing so, however, until you learn about two more basic points: the menu of investment choices available to you and the risk-return relationship.

BASIC POINT TWO

Focus on Four Investment Categories

While ignorance may be bliss, as the English poet Thomas Gray once wrote, it is not profitable. Before you begin to undertake my simple investment program, there are certain fundamental facts that you should be acquainted with.

Let's start at the very beginning. Basically, there are only four types of investment categories that you need to consider:

- Cash
- Bonds
- Common stocks; and
- Real estate

In this chapter, I'll tell you all you need to know about each of them before you start investing.

Note that I do not mention insurance, collectibles, or gold as investment categories. Insurance, as explained in Rule 3, should be treated as an essential protection rather than a way to make money. While collectibles—or "things," as I like to call them—often give their owners aesthetic pleasure, they do not yield benefit streams, such as dividend returns or interest payments. Moreover, they can be costly to store and protect. As for gold, it certainly does glitter from time to time and has long been considered a safe haven during times of international turmoil. It also shines beautifully in watches and jewelry. It is nevertheless a sterile investment in a rational world, as it earns neither interest nor dividends. And, like collectibles, it is costly to store and protect.

CASH

When investment professionals speak about cash, they don't literally mean the coins in your change purse or the paper currency in your wallet. To be sure, these items are certainly cash, but so too are a number of other instruments that can quickly be converted to currency. Cash, then, is defined as currency and checking deposits, plus any other short-term security that can be converted into currency on short notice and with no risk of loss of principal. Thus, a three-month Treasury bill (a very short term IOU from the government), which is just as safe as the currency issued by the government and which can be sold in the market at any time prior to its maturity at a relatively constant price, is considered to be cash just as much as the paper currency and metal coins that might be under your mattress. Also included in cash are bank savings deposits and any short-term bank certificates of deposit that can be converted to cash without penalty, all of which are guaranteed by the government up to $100,000. While not guaranteed in the same way, money-market mutual funds can also be considered equivalent to cash. They provide safety of principal and allow you to write large checks against them (usually in amounts in $250 or more). Consider them an interest-bearing checking account.

Every investor needs a cash reserve cushion to meet the various emergencies of life that always seem to come up at the most inconvenient times. One of my rules (Rule 3) will show you how to provide for such a cash reserve in the most efficient and cost-effective fashion.

Bonds

A bond is simply a long-term IOU. The original term of the borrowing is often twenty years or even longer. Bonds may be issued and/or guaranteed by the U.S. government (called a Treasury bond), a U.S. government agency such as the Government National Mortgage Association (called a Ginny Mae) or the Student Loan Marketing Association (called a Sallie Mae), corporations (called corporate bonds), or state or local governments or agencies (called municipal bonds). When you invest in a bond, you are lending money to the issuer. In return, you get a fixed periodic interest payment as well as a promise that the principal amount will be repaid at maturity—a date that is often years in the future.

You will often hear the interest payment referred to as the "coupon" payment. In olden days, bond investors actually clipped coupons from the bond and presented them to their banks to get their interest payments. Bonds are usually issued in denominations of $1,000. If the bond pays a yearly (coupon) interest payment of $70, the $70 interest payment is fixed for the life of the bond, and we say it has a yield of 7 percent. But market interest rates will vary with changes in economic activity and in the inflation rate. If rates go up to 8 percent so that newly issued $1,000 bonds of the same quality provide interest payments of $80 per year, then the bond paying $70 per year will have to fall in price to provide a competitive return. You wouldn't want to pay $1,000 for a bond paying $70 a year, when a new $1,000 bond was paying $80 a year! The $70 interest payment remains fixed so that when the bond falls in price, the effective yield becomes higher. The rule is: If interest rates rise, existing bonds fall in price. If interest rates fall, bonds rise in price. But if you hold until maturity, you will get your full $1,000 back from high-quality bonds, no matter what happens to interest rates in the interim. Some bonds don't provide periodic interest payments but rather are sold at a discount. They still pay the full $1,000 value at maturity, however, and the investor earns the difference between the purchase price and the value at maturity. These bonds are called zero coupon bonds.

Bonds are crucial instruments that help the central government pay for national defense, local governments repair roads, and corporations build factories. They are often called fixed-income investments because the bond buyer knows in advance the date and the amount of any interest payments. Sometimes, however, bondholders don't receive the promised payments because the issuer gets into financial difficulty. Federal government bonds are considered to be the safest since the federal government can always pay its interest. Municipal bonds are also relatively safe. Most municipal authorities have never defaulted on their obligations even during the toughest of economic times. Moreover, many municipal bonds are insured by a consortium of financial institutions and such bonds carry the highest investment grade.

Corporate bonds are somewhat riskier. While the bondholder has the first claim on the corporation's earnings and assets, corporate bonds can and have defaulted on their obligations. Most established blue-chip companies can be counted on to meet their obligations. But during the early 2000s, some very large companies such as WorldCom and Enron defaulted. For this reason, low-quality bonds need to promise significantly higher interest rates on their IOUs to induce investors to buy them. As we shall see, risk and return are closely related in our financial markets. Sometimes, these lower-quality bonds are called high-yield bonds or, more pejoratively, junk bonds.

High-quality bonds (and even diversified portfolios of somewhat lower quality ones) do provide investors with a reasonably steady source of income and can be particularly useful for retirees. They can also be useful for investors who need to provide for fixed future payments (such as college tuitions) and who want to provide some stability for their overall portfolio. The rules in this book show you how to determine the amount you should invest in bonds as well as how you can buy them efficiently at minimum cost.

Common Stocks

While bondholders are creditors of a company, stockholders are the actual owners. Without question, stocks were the hot-ticket items in the closing years of the twentieth century. Though many people viewed them as trading vehicles, common stocks represent an ownership interest.

If a company has 1,000 common shares outstanding and you own one share, you have an interest in 1/1,000 of the company's assets and earnings. And if the company declares a dividend, you will receive 1/1,000 of the amount declared. Although bondholders can never receive more than their promised interest payments, stockholders can gain increased returns if the company does especially well. Stocks are also called equity securities, but in my view they are more accurately called equity insecurities. You never know exactly what returns you will get from owning them.

Over long historical periods, stocks have provided investors with higher returns than bonds. Since the 1800s, stocks in the United States have provided investors with yearly returns between 8 and 9 percent while high-quality bond yields have averaged between 5 and 6 percent. Over the past seventy-five years, stocks have done even better, providing investors with average annual returns of about 10 percent. But stock returns have been far more volatile than bond yields. From March 2000 through October 2002, investors in a broadly diversified portfolio of stocks lost almost 45 percent of their investment. We economists tell our students, "There's no such thing as a free lunch." The extra returns from common stocks have come at the expense of considerable risk. As George Soros once said, if you are going "to be in the [stock-market] game, you have to endure the pain."

Unlike a bond, the buyer of a common stock receives no specific promises of payments in the future. As a part-owner of a firm, the buyer does share in the prosperity of the firm through dividend payments and, more important, through an increase in the value of the business. The greatest individual stock investments of the past have been companies such as IBM, Microsoft, Merck, and Johnson & Johnson—companies that have become leaders in their industry and that have enjoyed considerable growth over time. And that's where the opportunities and risks are involved. Stocks derive their value mainly from estimates of future growth—estimates that can never be made with any certainty. As Samuel Goldwyn once remarked, "Predictions are very difficult to make—especially about the future." Thus stocks can never have a precise value. At best, we can only expect stocks to fluctuate around some central tendency given by the best estimates that can be made concerning the company's future prospects.

For the most part, the stock market does a remarkably good job of pricing stocks efficiently so that they reflect the degree to which future growth is anticipated. The statistic used by individual investors and Wall Street professionals alike to judge how richly a stock is valued in the market is the price-earnings ratio. If a stock has earnings per share (the firm's total earnings divided by the number of shares outstanding) of $2 and it sells in the market at $40, it is said to have a price-earnings (P/E) ratio (or multiple) of 20 (40 ÷ 2). Stocks like eBay, for which very rapid future growth is forecast, tend to have very high P/Es or multiples, over 50. Mature companies, such as General Motors, tend to sell at low multiples, below 10. And our stock markets are generally extremely efficient in pricing stocks so that they reasonably reflect their differential future prospects.

But forecasting the future is extraordinarily difficult, and markets can make egregious mistakes. In the early 2000s, WorldCom sold at a very high multiple of reported earnings as enormous growth was anticipated in Internet traffic. Later, we learned that the company's earnings had been overstated. Moreover, overcapacity of fiber-optic networks led to such severe price competition that the growth of the Internet did not lead to a commensurate growth in WorldCom's revenues. WorldCom later declared bankruptcy. Still, in most periods and for most stocks, the market gets it right and is extraordinarily efficient in reflecting the differential long-term prospects for different companies with a remarkable degree of accuracy.

Bubbles in Stock Prices

Investors do need to know, however, that the stock market takes occasional trips to the loony bin. In Wall Street jargon, this is known as "Bubble Time." Such periods are often associated with the discovery of some innovative product, a new business opportunity, or an exciting new technology. Investors need to be aware that in the midst of some craze, people are often induced to plunge in and commit everything to the most outlandish investment ideas just when they shouldn't. Experience is the toughest kind of teacher—it gives you the test first and the lesson afterwards. Perhaps by learning a bit of history, you can assimilate the lesson vicariously without bearing the costs.

Every age appears to have had some peculiar investment folly where individuals, excited by the prospect of gain, get infected with an unreasoning herd mentality. It starts when investors begin to purchase a common stock or some other asset for no other reason than that its price is rising and other people are making money. As the economic historian Charles Kindleberger has stated, "There is nothing so disturbing to one's well-being and judgment as to see a friend get rich." And as Robert Shiller, author of the best-selling *Irrational Exuberance*, has noted, the process feeds on itself in a "positive feedback loop." A bubble starts when any asset begins to rise in price. The updraft encourages more people to buy, which in turn produces greater profits and induces a larger and larger group of participants. The whole mechanism is a kind of Ponzi scheme, where more and more credulous investors must be found to buy the assets from the earlier investors. Eventually one runs out of greater fools. We can illustrate the process with three speculative bubbles, the first from seventeenth-century Holland; the second from eighteenth-century England; and the last from late twentieth-century United States.

The Tulip-Bulb Craze

This classic bubble had nothing to do with the stock market at all; it was a full-scale speculative mania involving tulip bulbs. While tulip bulbs had been popular in Holland for years, the frenzy erupted when some bulbs became infected with a nonfatal virus that produced rather bizarre contrasting colored stripes. The Dutch highly valued these infected bulbs, and the more bizarre the bulb, the greater the cost of owning it. As prices rose, people began to view tulip bulbs as sound investments and prices rose even further, inducing more and more investors to enter the market. Charles MacKay, who chronicled the events in *Extraordinary Popular Delusions and the Madness of Crowds*, noted that the ordinary industry of the country was dropped in favor of speculation in tulip bulbs: "Nobles, citizens, farmers, mechanics, seamen, footmen, maid-servants, even chimney sweeps and old clothes women dabbled in tulips." Everyone imagined that the passion for tulips would last forever and that buyers from all over the world would come to Holland and pay whatever prices were asked for them.

At the height of the bubble, in early 1637, a single rare bulb sold for an amount equivalent to the price of a nobleman's castle. Apparently, as happens in all speculative crazes, prices eventually got so high that some people decided they would be prudent and sell their bulbs. Soon others followed suit. Like a snowball rolling downhill, bulb deflation grew at an increasingly rapid pace, and in no time at all, panic reigned. Down and down tulip-bulb prices went until most bulbs became almost worthless, bankrupting the thousands of speculators who imagined that wealth would be obtained so easily and painlessly.

The South Sea Bubble

Our next example took place in England nearly one hundred years later. In 1711, the South Sea Company was formed. The company helped restore faith in the government's credit worthiness by purchasing £10 million of government bonds. As a reward, the company was given a monopoly over all trade to the South Seas. There was great enthusiasm over the profits that might be made from trade with the New World, especially after the war between England and Spain ended. As word spread among investors about the fortunes to be made, the stock of the South Sea Company soared almost tenfold. The speculative craze was in full bloom.

Not even the South Sea Company was capable of handling the demands of all the fools who wanted to be parted from their money. Investors looked for other new ventures where they could get in on the ground floor. Just as speculators today search for the next Microsoft, so in England in the 1700s they looked for the next South Sea Company. Promoters obliged by organizing and bringing to the market a flood of new issues to meet the insatiable craving for investment.

As the days passed, new financing proposals ranged from ingenious to absurd—from importing a large number of jackasses from Spain (even though there was an abundant supply in England) to a new offering of a machine-gun company that promised to revolutionize the art of war. The machines could discharge both round bullets (to be used against Christians) and square ones (to be used against infidels). The prize, however, must surely go to the promoter who started "A company for carrying on an undertaking of great advantage, but nobody to know what it is."

As in all speculative manias, eventually the bubble popped, and investors suffered massive losses in most of the new issues of the period. Big losers in the South Sea Bubble included Isaac Newton, who exclaimed, "I can calculate the motions of heavenly bodies, but not the madness of people."

The Internet Craze

The biggest bubble of all time splattered in March 2000. During the next two and one-half years, over $7 trillion of market value evaporated. Indeed, comparing the Internet bubble to the tulip-bulb craze is undoubtedly unfair to the flowers. Most bubbles have been associated with some new technology or with some new business opportunity (as when profitable new trade opportunities spawned the South Sea Bubble). The Internet was associated with both: it represented a new technology, and it offered new business opportunities that promised to revolutionize the way consumers obtain information and purchase goods and services. The promise of the Internet spawned the largest creation and the largest destruction of wealth of all time.

Stocks of companies such as Amazon.com and Priceline .com—the drum majors of the Internet parade—rose to dizzying heights. Amazon, with relatively modest revenues from book sales and with large overall losses, sold at prices that made its total market capitalization (the price of its stock multiplied by the number of shares) larger than the total market values of all the publicly owned booksellers such as Barnes & Noble. Jeff Bezos, Amazon's CEO, was *Time* magazine's 1999 "Person of the Year." Priceline, an auction company whose site sold empty airline seats while losing buckets of money, sold at a total market capitalization that exceeded the capitalization of all the major airlines combined. Both stocks lost more than 90 percent of their value when the bubble popped.

There was such fascination with the Internet that companies that changed their names to include some Web orientation (such as .com or .net) doubled in price overnight. Investors were willing to throw their money at almost anything that claimed an Internet link. The volume of new issues during the period was unprecedented. And as was the case at the time of the South Sea Bubble, many companies that received financing were absurd. These ranged from a company called Digiscents (that offered a computer peripheral that would make Web sites smell) to ezboard.com (which produced Internet pages called toilet paper to help people "get the poop" on the Internet community). All became dot-com disasters.

But whatever the new issue, investors greeted it with hurrahs and fistfuls of cash, even when the company had neither earnings nor even sales. In previous bubbles, new issues would rise by what was considered in the Internet era a paltry 25 or 50 percent. In the New Economy era, some

IPOs soared 500 percent or more. VA Linux rose over 730 percent in its first day of trading, to almost $200 per share. In 2002, the company clung to life at less than a dollar a share.

Wall Street's high-profile securities analysts provided much of the hot air floating the Internet bubble. Analysts such as Mary Meeker, Henry Blodgett, and Jack Grubman became household names and were accorded the status of sports heroes or rock stars. Meeker was dubbed by *Barron's* magazine the "Queen of the 'Net.'" Blodgett was known as "King Henry," while Grubman acquired the sobriquet "Telecom Guru" and was considered almost a "demigod." In fact, these analysts were being paid to be bullish rather than to be accurate. By promising continued favorable coverage of the investment banking clients of the securities firms, their real function was to bring lucrative banking fees to their firms, not to provide accurate advice to investors.

The media also contributed a continuous supply of hot air for floating the Internet bubble. Across the world, health clubs, airports, bars, and restaurants were permanently tuned into CNBC. The stock market was a hotter story than sex. Even Howard Stern would interrupt more usual discussions about porn queens and body parts to muse about the stock market and then to tout some particular Internet stocks. And, unfortunately, the speculative climate encouraged a string of business scandals that shook the capitalist system to its roots.

What Lessons Should We Learn?

Most of the time the stock market does an excellent job of insuring that stock prices accurately reflect the real value of the corporations they represent. Why, then, do I tell you these stories of the occasional times when the stock market is less than rational and efficient? Because it is precisely at these times that individuals get swept up in the speculative frenzy and make mistakes that can ruin their financial future.

I am going to recommend some simple, low-risk, diversified (even boring) strategies that can assure you a comfortable retirement. Yet countless individuals who may have owned such diversified portfolios found it impossible to stay the course when their neighbors boasted of an Internet stock that doubled during the previous week. Out went the portfolio—to be replaced by a dangerous concentration in new fad stocks that fizzled out all too soon. Inexorably, all excessively exuberant markets succumb to the laws of gravity. The consistent losers in the market, from my personal experience, are those who are unable to resist being swept up in some kind of tulip-bulb craze and who bet their entire stake on a single stock or a single industry. The ability to avoid such horrendous mistakes by diversifying over many types of stocks and over several asset classes is probably the most important factor in preserving one's capital and allowing it to grow. The lesson is so obvious and yet so easy to ignore.

Real Estate

In owning your own home, you are by default a real estate investor. Indeed, for many people, the bulk of their wealth is concentrated in this asset category—one that has proven to be a very lucrative investment in recent years. It offers significant tax advantages and the opportunity to profit from rising house prices. You should never pay rent to others when you can pay yourself instead through mortgage installments. If the value of your home constitutes the total amount of your overall wealth, read no further. You are already fully invested in this asset category.

If, however, you find that the value of your home is only a fraction of your bond and stock portfolios, you might want to broaden your assets by buying commercial real estate. This type of real estate offers an advantage that individual home ownership does not: a steady and often generous stream of income. By commercial real estate, I mean properties such as office buildings, shopping malls, apartment buildings, and so forth.

Until the past twenty years or so, ordinary investors just didn't have sufficient cash to participate in such transactions. Enter the relatively new medium of real estate investment trusts. Known as REITs (pronounced "Reets," which rhymes with "beets"), real estate investment trusts own portfolios of properties. They issue ownership shares in these properties, and that's where you come in. You can buy shares in the portfolio rather than owning an entire building or shopping center. The shares trade like ordinary common stocks, with most being offered on the New York Stock Exchange.

Thus, REITs are similar to mutual funds. And just as mutual funds often concentrate in categories such as short-term bonds or growth stocks, REITs are frequently organized by certain property types. For example, there are apartment house REITs, which own portfolios of multi-family housing units. There are also office building REITs, as well as real estate trusts specializing in hotels, shopping malls, and warehouses. There are even "jailhouse REITs" that own prisons. If one wanted to buy a diversified portfolio of all property types, one would need to purchase a mutual fund that owned a wide selection of REIT shares.

Although long-term data on REIT returns are not available, it appears that, in recent years, REITs have generated returns very similar to those provided by common stocks in general. They usually provide generous dividend yields and often exhibit more stability than other equity securities. And, real estate returns don't always move in lockstep with other assets. For example, during periods of accelerating inflation, properties tend to do much better than other common stocks and bonds. Thus, adding real estate to a portfolio tends to reduce its overall volatility.

But real estate prices have also been subject to speculative crazes that are among the more spectacular bubbles in asset prices. In the late 1980s in Japan, real estate prices began a phenomenal increase with no top in sight. Land values in Tokyo had risen so high that the land under the Imperial Palace was valued at more than all the real estate in California. The Japanese even bought up important "trophy properties" in the United States, such as the Pebble Beach Golf Course and Rockefeller Center, at exorbitant prices. Financial publications at the time boasted, "You ain't seen nothing yet." Again, we learned that the most dangerous words in the English language that investors can hear are, "This time is different."

BASIC POINT THREE

Understand the Risk/Return Relationship

One of the most enduring truths about financial markets is that risk and return are related. By risk I mean the possibility of suffering harm or loss. If you buy a one-year Treasury bill to yield 3 percent, you can be certain that you will earn exactly 3 percent, because that rate is guaranteed by the U.S. government. But if you buy a common stock with the expectation of receiving a 3 percent dividend yield and some growth in the price of the shares, you could be very disappointed. The dividend could be cut and the price of the shares could fall rather than rise. Investment risk is the chance that expected returns will not materialize and that the securities you hold will fall in price. In general, there is no such thing as a free lunch. In order to induce investors into buying risky securities, a higher return must be offered. Thus, higher investment returns can only be achieved by accepting greater risk.

RISK AND RETURNS FOR DIFFERENT ASSET CLASSES: 1926–2002

	HISTORICAL RETURNS *Average Annual Rate of Return (percent)*	RISK INDICATOR *Range of Annual Returns (percent)*
Cash (Treasury bills, etc.)	3–4	plus 1 to plus 9
Long-term bonds (corporate)	6	minus 5 to plus 15
Common stocks	10	minus 27 to plus 52

Source: Ibbotson Associates.

The table above illustrates the relationship between risk and return in United States markets over a 75-year period. Real estate is absent from this chart because there are no comparable long-run data for this time period. Real estate returns for periods for which we have data have been similar to the returns from common stocks. Common stocks have been the big winner, providing an average annual return of about 10 percent. This 10 percent return includes both the dividends and capital gains resulting from growth over time in corporate earnings and dividends. But these generous returns have been achieved at the expense of considerable annual volatility, which is a good indicator of risk. In some years, stocks have lost more than a quarter of their value. And sometimes there have been three years in a row of negative returns, as was the case from 2000 through 2002.

In fact, equity investors have suffered through several severe bear markets over the past fifty years. The chart below shows the magnitude of the declines as well as the number of months it took the stock market to recover. Note that the bear market of the early millennium was one of the sharpest and longest of the post–World War II period, as stocks lost 45 percent of their value. Note also that it took over five years for the market to recover from the similar sharp decline of 1973–74. Investors today have vivid recent memories of the risks of equity investing and the carnage suffered by their portfolios. There are some things in life you just have to bear, like traffic jams, telemarketers, and meddling in-laws. Unfortunately, if you are an equity investor, from time to time bear markets are unavoidable as well.

THE SIZE AND SHAPE OF BEAR MARKETS
MAJOR S&P 500 DECLINES: 1953–2002

	THE EXTENT OF THE DECLINE		MONTHS TO RECOVER*	
Year	*%*	*Months*	*75% of Decline**	*100% of Decline**
1957	20	3	11	12
1961–62	29	6	10	14
1966	22	9	5	6
1968–70	37	18	9	22
1973–74	48	21	20#	64
1981–82	22	13	2	3
1987	34	2	18##	24
1990	20	3	5	5
2000–02†	45	31	—	—
Average	29	9	10	19

* From market low
# 50% of decline recovered in 5 months
##50% of decline recovered in 12 months
† Decline through October, 2002, not included in average

Source: E. D. Everett, "Making Sense of Market Unpredictability," *Babson Staff Letter*, August 30, 2002.

Fortunately, the stock market does tend to rise most of the time. When market returns are measured over five- and ten-year periods, we see that the trend is predominantly up—even during the ten-year period ending in

2002. And over ten-year investment periods, stocks have usually provided considerably higher investment returns than those available from bonds (although bonds did do better over the decade ending in 2002). Still, if you want to shoot for the higher gains that usually come from buying stocks, you will have to endure the pain of suffering through occasional periods of sharp losses.

THE MARKET'S UPWARD BIAS
S&P 500—PERIOD RETURNS 1926–2002

Time Periods	*Advances*	*Declines*
1 year	70%	30%
5 years	90%	10%
10 years	97%	3%

Source: Ibbotson Associates.

Long-term high-quality bonds have provided an average annual return of 6 percent. The range of annual returns is much narrower than is the case for stocks and the possibility of loss is much smaller than for common stocks. But there have been some years in which investors lost money in the bond market when bond prices fell more than was offset by the promised interest payments. For example, in the early 1980s, a portfolio of U.S. Treasury bonds lost almost 10 percent. Still, a bad year for bonds is like a day at the beach when compared to the kinds of losses suffered by stock investors.

Safest of all, in terms of price fluctuation, are cash investments. Even during periods of very low interest rates, cash has never provided a negative dollar return. But even cash investments have a degree of risk associated with them. "Inflation" is the term used to describe the universal risk associated with every financial form, even cash. Simply put, it means that money never has a constant value. And throughout recent history, the dollars we use for our financial transactions have become less valuable with each passing year. As the following table shows, the rate at which the dollar declines fluctuates widely.

THE VALUE OF A DOLLAR IN SELECTED TIME PERIODS

Time Period	*Value at Start*	*Value at End*
1967–71	$1.00	$0.84
1977–81	$1.00	$0.69
1987–91	$1.00	$0.84
1997–2001	$1.00	$0.92

Thus, even those who believe in stuffing money into the proverbial mattress face the risk that the money will be less valuable when they take it out. The returns that you hope to receive from any investment are always influenced by the level of inflation. Of course, inflation has even more devastating effects on a bond portfolio. Not only does the real value of the fixed-income payments fall during inflationary times, but bondholders suffer a double whammy. When inflation is rampant, interest rates have to rise to entice buyers to hold bonds. In 1981, for example, when inflation soared to almost 10 percent, even U.S. Treasury bonds had double-digit yields. But as yields rose, the prices of existing bonds fell, subjecting holders to punishing capital losses.

Of the four asset categories, only real estate tends to shine when inflation accelerates. And common stocks also protect investors over the long run from high inflation, although, like bonds, they tend to do poorly over the short run when inflation accelerates. All this suggests that a sensible portfolio should consist of more than one asset type. But that brings us to the how-to-do-it part of the book.

Now that you have fired your investment adviser, are focused on the four major investment classes available, and appreciate the relationship between risk and return, you are ready to learn the ten basic rules for achieving financial security.

Part Two

THE RULES

The advice in this book is both simple and realistic. There is no magic potion in the investment world because the truth is that one doesn't exist. There is no quick road to riches. And if someone promises you a path to overnight riches, cover your ears and close your pocketbook. If an investment idea seems too good to be true, it is too good to be true. What I offer are ten simple, time-tested rules that can build wealth and provide retirement security. Think of the rules as the proven way to get rich slowly.

Much of the financial advice offered to consumers is unnecessarily fancy and complex. I am reminded of one of the favorite stories of a teacher of mine, Jack Viner. Viner would tell of a woman who was purchasing a water bowl for her dog. The clerk asked, "Would you like me to inscribe the word 'dog' on the side of the bowl?" The woman answered, "Oh, that won't be necessary. My husband doesn't drink water and my dog can't read." My rules are unadorned and easy to follow. I promise you that these simple rules are all the investment advice you will ever need.

RULE ONE

Start Saving Now, Not Later: Time Is Money

THE AMOUNT of capital you start with is not nearly as important as getting started early. Procrastination is the natural assassin of opportunity. Every year you put off investing makes your ultimate retirement goals more difficult to achieve. Trust in time rather than timing. As a sign in the window of a bank put it, little by little you can safely stock up a strong reserve here, *but not until you start.*

The secret of getting rich slowly (but surely) is the miracle of compound interest. Albert Einstein once described compound interest as the "greatest mathematical discovery of all time." It may sound complicated, but it simply involves earning a return not only on your original investment but also on the accumulated interest that you reinvest.

Returns Throughout U.S. History

Jeremy Siegel, the author of an excellent investing book entitled *Stocks for the Long Run,* has calculated the returns from a variety of financial assets from 1800 through 2002. His work shows the incredible power of compounding. One dollar invested in stocks since 1802 would have accumulated to almost $7 million by the end of 2002. This amount far outdistanced the rate of inflation as measured by the Consumer Price Index (CPI). The figure below also shows the much more modest returns that have been achieved by U.S. Treasury bills and gold.

Total Return Indices

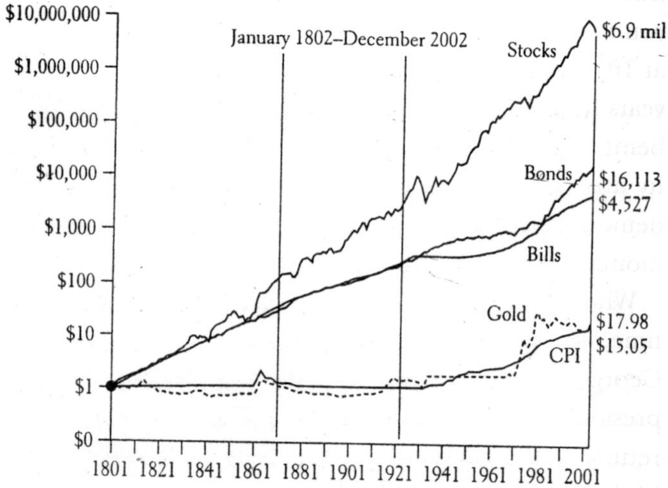

Source: Jeremy J. Siegel, *Stocks for the Long Run,* reprinted by permission and updated by Professor Siegel.

The Miracle of Compound Interest

Why is compounding so powerful? Suppose you open up a $100 savings account that pays interest at 10 percent per year. After one year, the account will be worth $110—the original $100 plus the $10 of interest that was earned. Now the second year, the interest earned will be $11 rather than $10. By leaving the first $10 on deposit, interest will be earned on $110. Thus, at the end of two years, you will have $121 rather than $120, and at the end of three years, you will have $133.10. At the end of ten years, you will have almost $260, $60 more than if you had earned only $10 per year interest. This is the magic of compound interest.

There is a handy rule that can tell you how long it will take to double your money if you invest it at compound interest. It is called the rule of 72. Take the rate of return you will earn from an investment and divide it into the number 72. The result is the number of years it will take you to double your money. For example, if you can invest at 10 percent, as in my previous example, it will take 7.2 years for your money to double (72 ÷ 10). As this book is being written, corporate bonds of investment-grade quality are yielding 7.2 percent. Thus, we can conveniently demonstrate that it would take ten years to double your money at that rate (72 ÷ 7.2 = 10).

When money is left to compound for long periods of time, the resulting accumulations can be awe-inspiring. If George Washington had taken one dollar from his first presidential salary and invested it at 8 percent, the rate of return on common stocks over the past two hundred years, his heirs today would have about $8 million.

Todd Grady reminds us of an actual case involving Benjamin Franklin. When Franklin died in 1791, he left a gift of $5,000 to each of his two favorite cities, Boston and Philadelphia. A stipulation of the gift was that the money could only be paid out at two specific dates, one hundred and two hundred years after the date of the gift. After one hundred years, each city could withdraw $500,000 for public works projects. In two hundred years, each city could withdraw whatever balance was left. In 1991, after two hundred years, each city received approximately $20 million. Franklin's point was to teach all of us in a dramatic way how powerful compounding can be. As Franklin liked to describe the process, the benefits of compounding are that "The money that money makes, makes money."

The classic example of compounding involves the purchase of Manhattan Island in 1626. We often hear that the Native Americans who sold Manhattan for $24 were rooked by the white men. In fact, the error was in not investing the money wisely. Had the $24 been invested at a 10 percent return, it would be worth almost $100 trillion today—an amount considerably more than the value of all the much-improved New York real estate.

The Million-Dollar Difference

A problem that I give my finance students demonstrates the importance of starting sooner rather than later. Indeed, within the numbers below lies the most important investing principle of all. Put time on your side—it's never too early to invest for retirement.

> William and James are twin brothers who are 65 years old. Forty-five years ago (at the end of the year when he reached age 20), William started an Individual Retirement Account (IRA), and put $2,000 in the account at the end of each year. After twenty years of contributions, William stopped making new deposits but left the accumulated contributions in the IRA fund. The fund produced returns

of 10 percent per year tax-free. James started his own IRA when he reached age 40 (just after William quit) and contributed $2,000 per year for twenty-five years, making his last contribution today. James invested 25 percent more money in total than William. James also earned 10 percent on his investments tax-free.

(a) What are the values of William's and James's IRA funds today?

(b) What personal finance lesson does this exercise suggest?

The answers are usually a big surprise to my students. The value of William's IRA today is almost $1.25 million. The value of James's IRA is less than $200,000. Even though James put much more money into his retirement plan, William's stake was more than a million dollars larger. William wins the race hands down. The moral is clear: you can accumulate more money just by starting now.

I could run through other examples involving actual returns in the stock market. One investor might start early and have the worst possible timing by investing at the top of the market each year. Another investor starts later but is the world's luckiest investor, buying at the absolute bottom of the market every year. The investor who started early, even though she may have invested only half the money and had the worst timing possible, accumulates much more money. Luck in picking the right time to invest is all well and good, but time is far more important than timing. There is always a good excuse to put off planning for retirement. Don't let it happen to you. Put time on your side.

If you want a get-rich-quick investment strategy, this is not the book for you. I'll leave that for the snake oil salesmen. You can only get poor quickly. To get rich, you will have to do it slowly, and you have to start now.

RULE TWO

Keep a Steady Course: The Only Sure Road to Wealth Is Regular Savings

A WIDELY HELD belief is that the tickets to a comfortable retirement and a fat investment portfolio are instructions on how to allocate your assets and what extraordinary individual stocks or mutual funds you should buy. Unfortunately, these tickets are not even worth the paper they are printed on. The harsh truth is that the most important driver in the growth of your assets is how much you save, and saving requires discipline. Without a regular savings program, it doesn't matter if you make 5 percent, 10 percent, or even 15 percent on your investment funds. The single most important thing you can do to achieve financial security is to begin a regular savings program and to start it as early as possible. The only reliable route to a comfortable retirement is to build up a nest egg slowly and steadily. Yet few people follow this basic rule. The nonprofit organization Public Agenda reported in the late 1990s that almost half of Americans between the ages of twenty-two and sixty-one had saved less than $10,000 for their retirement. Most Americans are woefully unprepared financially to enjoy the longer and healthier life expectancy that is possible today.

SAVVY SAVINGS TIPS

I can hear the chorus of complaints already: "Sure it would be great to save more money but I can't make ends meet as it is." As the old saying goes, "It's not hard to meet expenses . . . they're everywhere." Many people have found that the following techniques have helped to trick themselves into saving more.

1. Pay Yourself First

The best way to ensure that you don't spend every nickel of every paycheck is to set up a plan so that you never get your hands on the money in the first place. You can do this by establishing a payroll deduction plan where you work. Under such plans, money is subtracted from your paycheck before you receive it and automatically put into a retirement fund. This not only leads to regular savings but also offers lucrative tax advantages. As we will see in the next rule, each dollar put into a 401(k) retirement plan (up to certain limits) is not taxable. If you are in the 35 percent tax bracket, a dollar paid out to you only nets you 65 cents of spendable income. A dollar put into a 401(k) plan nets you a dollar. Think of it as saving 65 cents and having the U.S. Treasury contribute 35 cents to your retirement fund. Moreover, many companies will match (or at least partially match) any contributions you make to the plan. If so, a dollar put into the plan will generate an additional dollar of investable funds in your retirement plan. If you are not contributing to your company's retirement plan, you are missing out on the very best way to build a retirement nest egg.

2. Find a Save More Tomorrow Plan

Two economists, Richard Thaler and Shlomo Benartzi, who combine the teachings of psychology and economics, have come up with a brilliant way to increase employees' participation rates in their retirement plans. Normally, that is not easy to do. If one asks an employee who has become used to a particular level of take-home pay to increase his allocation to a retirement plan by one dollar, he will view the resulting deduction (even though it is less than a dollar because the bigger deduction reduces taxes) as a loss of current spending availability. The psychologist Daniel Kahneman, who won the Nobel Prize in Economics in 2002, has shown that individuals weigh these losses much more heavily than gains. Estimates have been made suggesting that losses hurt roughly twice as much as gains give pleasure. When this loss aversion is coupled with how difficult it is to exhibit self-control and how easy it is to procrastinate, the psychologists teach us that it is perfectly understandable why people tend to save too little.

Thaler and Benartzi's "Save More Tomorrow Plan" is designed to help those employees who would like to save more but lack the willpower to act on that desire. The essence of the plan is to have employees commit in advance to allocate a portion of any salary increases toward retirement saving. If employees join the plan, their contribution to their savings retirement plan is increased, beginning with the first paycheck after a raise. This feature mitigates the perceived loss aversion of a cut in take-home pay. The contribution rate continues to increase on each scheduled raise until it reaches the maximum tax-deductible contribution to the plan allowed by law. In this way, inertia and status quo bias work toward keeping people in the plan. The employee is allowed to opt out of the plan at any time.

Thaler and Benartzi first implemented their plan in 1998 at a midsize manufacturing company. The company was suffering from low participation in its savings retirement plan at the time. The Save More Tomorrow Plan proved to be very popular. More than three quarters of the employees of the firm agreed to join. Moreover, over 80 percent of those employees stayed with it through subsequent pay raises. Even those who withdrew did not reduce their contribution rates to the original levels; they merely stopped the future increases from taking place. So even these workers were saving significantly more than they were before joining the plan.

Although these kinds of experiments are just beginning at companies, nothing should stop you from going to the human resources department where you work and creating such a plan on your own. If you are not contributing now or if your contribution rate is very low, you could just say, "I'd like to have one half [or any other percent you wish] of my raise go into the company's savings retirement plan." You could not do yourself a bigger favor.

3. Make Out a Budget

Without question, monitoring your expenses is boring. It is also frequently shocking.

Should you carefully monitor your expenditures for

some period of time, you are likely to discover how much money you are wasting or spending on things you believe are unimportant. Benjamin Franklin once said, "Beware of small expenses, a small leak will sink a great ship." And I'll bet that such monitoring would also lead you to discover that there are some very simple things you can do to reduce your monthly expenditures.

Even if you don't wish to make a formal budget, it would be a good idea just to keep track of every dollar you spend for two or three months. Make a note of the extra pair of shoes, the video you bought but only looked at once, the CDs, the sweater that looked neat, and so forth. The *Motley Fool Investment Guide* then suggests that you put your purchases into two categories: the things you really needed and the things you just wanted at the time. Then look really hard at the second category. You are likely to find yourself among those who are buying much more than they need each month, things that get used once and then just clutter up the house. As the *Motley Fool Guide* puts it, "Most of our houses in America are simply overloaded with unnecessary *stuff.*"

4. Change a Spending Habit or Two

Suppose you are a movie buff, like I am, and you and your partner see one movie a week. The weekly expenditure might look something like this:

Two movie tickets	$ 15.00
Large tub of popcorn	5.00
Two large sodas	6.00
Gas to movie theater	3.00
Total expense	$ 29.00

Now consider once every four weeks renting a movie instead and making your own popcorn. (Cover the bottom of a pan with olive oil, heat the oil, put in three kernels, when they pop, cover the bottom with kernels, put a cover on the pan, pop, and then salt to taste. It tastes much better than movie popcorn.) The expenditures every four weeks would be as follows:

Movie rental fee	$ 4.00
Liter of soda	1.00
Olive oil and popcorn	1.00
Total expense	$ 6.00

Thus, every four weeks (thirteen times a year) you will save $23, or about $300 per year.

How about a big-ticket item that costs you a bundle? Do you really need to drive the latest model car every year or so? I've got a five-year-old car that runs like a top, and my mother-in-law owns one that is eighteen years old and still perfectly comfortable and serviceable. By keeping your cars somewhat longer, you can easily save thousands of dollars a year even after considering the extra maintenance that older cars require.

5. Think in Terms of Opportunity Costs

Economists tend to think of the real cost of anything as what you give up to get it. If I'm hungry and have two bucks in my pocket and I'm in McDonald's, I know that the real cost of the Chicken McNuggets I order is the Big Mac I could be enjoying. Extend this kind of reasoning to what you will have to give up in retirement when you spend an extra dollar today.

Take the previous example of renting the movie every four weeks rather than going out to a theater. We saw that by so doing it was possible to save $300 a year. Now, instead of thinking of the opportunity cost of having another $300 to spend each year on something else, envision it as having $15,000 more in twenty years or a staggering extra $90,000 in forty years. Remember the lesson in Rule 1: Time is money. Three hundred dollars a year invested at 8 percent grows to about $90,000 in forty years. And if you are twenty-five years old today, the real cost of going out to the movies one extra time a month is the ability to have an enormous additional sum in retirement.

6. Be Saving in Your Spending

Do you just throw away the coupon booklets in the Sunday newspapers? Why not use them and then put away the dollars that you save from using them? How about visiting those discount retailers with slogans like "An educated consumer is our best customer." First-rate brand name items are available at these places at substantial savings. And for some big-ticket items, have you tried the Internet to get the best deal? A dollar saved is more than a dollar earned because taxes reduce any earnings to far less than a dollar.

Jonathan Clements, who writes an excellent personal finance column for the *Wall Street Journal*, invited his readers to tell him the smartest financial moves they made to save a few bucks. Here is an example of some the messages he received.*

*"Methods Readers Employ to Make and Save Money" by Jonathan Clements. Copyright 1999 by Dow Jones & Company, Inc. Reproduced with permission of Dow Jones & Company, Inc.

- My wife and I take the change out of our pockets at the end of the day and put it into our daughter's piggy bank. At the end of the month, we have $50 or more, and we stick it into a mutual fund that will pay for her college education.
—Mark Gabriella, St. Louis, Missouri

- I always cringe whenever we go out to eat and the three kids order soft drinks. We all know the margins on those. Therefore, I made a deal: The kids have the option of either ordering a soft drink or ordering water and receiving a dollar from me. The results have been great, especially on vacations when all meals are eaten out. The benefits are threefold: The money stays in the family, the kids learn to forego present gratification, and water is healthier for them.
—Mike Giangardella, Warren, Ohio

- After I finished paying off my car loan, I made a vow to myself that I would never make car payments again. So after the loan was satisfied in 1990, I started investing the same $500 per month. Today, it is worth over $100,000. —Bill Wilson, Dallas, Texas

7. *Pay Off Your Credit Card Balance*

Scott Adams, creator of the *Dilbert* comic strip, calls credit cards the crack cocaine of the financial world. "They start out as a no-fee . . . way to get instant gratification, but the next thing you know you're freebasing shoes at Nordstrom's." Keeping a balance on your credit card is about the worst financial move you can make.

The first place to put extra savings is toward paying off your credit card balance. By reducing and eventually eliminating the high monthly interest charges, you can finally begin to get ahead of the game.

Jack Brennan, the chief executive officer of the Vanguard Group, gives the following example in his investment guide, *Straight Talk on Investing.*

> Suppose your various credit card balances have ballooned to $20,000. At a 1.5% monthly interest rate, you're being charged $300 a month in interest. The card companies may require you to pay only a total of $500 each month, because they're in no hurry to have you reduce your debt burden. But now let's say that you get a raise of, say, $120 a month. That might push up your take-home pay by $80 or so, after taxes and retirement plan contributions. If you apply that $80 to your credit card payments—perhaps using automatic bill-paying to make sure you do so—you'll have cut the balance by an *extra* $960 in 12 months. As a bonus for paying down that extra $960, your monthly interest charges will drop by nearly $15—more than $170 a year and you'll make progress in paying off the debt.

Strategies for Catching Up

Suppose you did not do the things you should have when you were younger and now you find yourself in your fifties with essentially no savings, no retirement plan, and burdensome credit card debts.

This is the sad fate of too many in what is known as the Boomer generation—the millions who were born between 1946 and 1964 and who are now heading into the retirement years with much of what savings they did have wiped out in the aftermath of the Internet bubble. What do you do now? It's going to be a lot harder to plan for a comfortable retirement and it will require a good deal more discipline. But it's never too late to make a plan. The following suggestions should help you meet your goal.

1. Downsize Your Lifestyle and Start Saving Now

There is no other way to make up for lost time than to start a rigorous program of savings now. You have no other choice than to be frugal. You simply have to trade in your $3 morning cappuccino for a simple dollar cup of Joe. You could consider selling your large house and moving into a simpler, less expensive place. You may even want to move to a less expensive location where living costs and taxes will be lower. You don't have easy choices now, but with discipline you can make up for lost time.

We will talk about taxes in the next rule, but you should know that Congress has made catching up a bit easier. It is now possible for investors over fifty to make extra contributions to their tax-advantaged retirement plans. Older investors who have employer-sponsored 401(k) or 403(b) or individual retirement plans, for example, can make extra contributions that will ensure that all of the earnings from your investments accumulate tax-free.

2. Consider Pushing Retirement Back a Few Years

If you are still in the workforce, you may have no other choice but to push back your retirement date. A comfortable early retirement will be unattainable. With longer and healthier life expectations, this alternative may not be as unpleasant as you imagine. By postponing retirement to normal retirement age, you can fatten up your Social Security benefits. It will also give you a few more years to contribute to your retirement plans and give whatever savings you have more time to grow. And, by working a few years longer, you may be better able to repay car loans and mortgages and thus further improve your cash flow in retirement.

3. Make the Most of Your Home Equity

If you own a home, consider unlocking its value. As this book is being written, mortgage rates are at their lowest levels in over forty years. If you have not refinanced your home, do so now. With long-term mortgage rates below 6 percent in early 2003, you can slash your monthly payments and put the savings to work in your investment portfolio. If you have a home and any expensive credit card debt, pay off the card balance with a home equity loan. Finally, if you are retired and have considerable equity in your home, you might consider a "reverse mortgage" where, over time, you assume larger and larger mortgage debt and use the proceeds for living expenses. Of course, this is not saving, but it may be the only way for you to meet expenses.

Retirement Planning

Do you know whether your savings plans and investment portfolio will be adequate, together with Social Security, to provide you with a comfortable retirement? If you are not sure, you don't have to have an expensive financial planner to get help. A host of Internet sites exist that can give solid advice and analysis either free of charge or for a nominal fee. These sites can help you determine if your present situation is likely to meet your retirement goals. If you are not on track, the programs will suggest ways by which you can steer a path to where you want to be. Some of the sites that will help those who are not computer challenged are listed in the box below.

Web Sites to Help in Financial Planning

www.fidelity.com
A link exists to the Fidelity "Planning Center" where you can access planning and retirement worksheets

www.morningstar.com
You can register as a user and get some retirement tools and worksheets free

www.troweprice.com
A link to Investment Planning and Tools can be accessed without cost

www.vanguard.com
Vanguard customers can access a service from Financial Engines for a fee of $150

None of the Web sites listed here can guarantee that you will meet your goals. But what they can point out is whether your current savings plan and your investment allocation are likely to lead to a comfortable retirement or a future diet of birdseed. They can give you a reasonable idea of whether you are saving enough for retirement. The rest is up to you.

The Millionaire Next Door

If some of the above suggestions sound totally unreal or Draconian, consider the work of Thomas Stanley and William Danko, authors of a best-selling book, *The Millionaire Next Door.* The book describes a twenty-year study of the wealthy in America and how they got that way. Stanley and Danko began by interviewing people in upscale neighborhoods and from these interviews made a remarkable discovery: Most people who live in expensive homes and drive luxury cars do not have much wealth. They discovered something else even stranger: Many very wealthy people don't live in fancy houses in exclusive neighborhoods. Nor have they earned advanced degrees or inherited lots of money or hit the jackpot with some lucky investment. Wealth is more often the result of a lifestyle of hard work and the discipline of regular savings.

What was at first surprising to the authors was that many of the millionaires they surveyed did not appear to be rich. They did not wear thousand-dollar Italian suits, or Rolex watches, and they did not drive current-model imported luxury cars. They typically did not receive any inheritance—they were first-generation affluent. These people didn't look like millionaires. They lived below their means, but that did not mean completely sacrificing comfortable living. Nor did it mean simply accumulating wealth for the sake of wealth alone and foregoing any of the tangible benefits that come with earning a reasonable income. But it did mean that they had the discipline to budget and control their expenses, and they regularly put aside some of their income toward saving and investment.

You aren't what you drive, admonish Stanley and Danko.

One Internet reviewer of the book suggested that it is not true that the stereotypical person discussed by the authors is an unhappy, penny-pinching miser who never enjoys his wealth. He wrote:

> I don't want to hang out at the country club showing off to a bunch of four flushers who are up to their eyeballs in mortgages and credit card debt. Getting up in the morning and knowing that there is no mortgage on the house, every bill is paid IN FULL and on time, is the most wonderful feeling in the world. It is a lot better than buying a $5,000 watch that will be used only to impress someone in a $1200 suit. I do take great family vacations, go to dinner a few times a month and mow my own lawn. I do not deprive myself of anything I really want. I just don't want the latest things that are being peddled on TV. Buying these at full price would only make a sucker out of me. There are things you need, and things you want, and it's OK to treat yourself but you must keep a strong grip on what you are buying and why you are buying it.

For those obsessed with the accumulation of material things, La Rochefoucauld had it sized up in the seventeenth century: "Before desiring something passionately, one should inquire into the happiness of the man who possesses it."

Jack Brennan took a look at shareowners who owned more than $1 million of Vanguard's mutual funds. He found that the millionaires in the Vanguard family were much like those interviewed by Stanley and Danko. To be sure, there were the business executives and celebrities you would expect to find in such a group. But Brennan also found that Vanguard's millionaire investors included many people of modest incomes such as teachers, office workers, oil rig workers, and telephone line repair people. He concluded: "Quite simply, they have been very disciplined savers."

So there are the first two rules: Put time on your side. Start saving early and save regularly. Live modestly and don't touch the money that's been set aside. If you need further discipline, remember that the only thing worse than being dead is to outlive the money you have put aside for retirement. And if projections are to be believed, about 1 million of today's baby boomers will live to be at least a hundred.

RULE THREE

Don't Be Caught Empty-Handed: Insurance and Cash Reserves

Remember Murphy's Law: What can go wrong will go wrong. And don't forget O'Toole's commentary: Murphy was an optimist. Bad things do happen to good people. Life is a risky proposition, and unexpected financial needs occur in everyone's lifetime. The boiler tends to blow up just at the time that your family incurs whopping medical expenses. A job layoff happens just after your son has totaled the family car. That's why every family needs a cash reserve as well as adequate insurance to cope with the catastrophes of life.

Establishing a Cash Reserve

I know many brokers will tell you not to miss investing opportunities by sitting on your cash. "Cash is trash" is the mantra of the brokerage community. But everyone needs to keep some reserves in safe and liquid investments to pay for an unexpected medical bill or to provide a cushion during a time of unemployment. Assuming that you are protected by medical and disability insurance at work, this reserve might be established to cover three months of looming expenses. Moreover, any large future expenditures (such as your daughter's college tuition bill) should be funded with short-term investments (such as a bank certificate of deposit) whose maturity matches the date on which the funds will be needed. In this rule, we'll learn how to establish such a reserve as efficiently as possible, using one or more of the following instruments.

Money-Market Mutual Funds

I believe that money-market mutual funds (or money funds) provide the best instrument for investors to park their cash reserves. They combine safety, relatively generous yields, and the ability to write large checks against your fund balance, generally in amounts of at least $250. Interest earnings continue until the checks clear. Interest rates on these funds have ranged from 1 to 5 percent during the decade of the 1990s and early 2000s. Not all money-market funds are created equal, however; some have significantly higher expense ratios (the costs of running and managing the funds) than others. In general, lower expenses mean higher returns for you. A sample of relatively low expense funds is presented in the table below.

Some Low-Expense Money-Market Funds

Fund Name	*Minimum Initial Purchase ($)*	*Minimum Amount for Check Withdrawal*	*Recent Expense Ratio (2002)*
Fidelity Spartan Money Market Fund www.fidelity.com 800-343-3548	$20,000	$1,000	0.42%
TIAA-CREF Money Market Fund www.tiaa-cref.com 800-223-1200	2,500	250	0.29%
USAA Money Market Fund www.usaa.com 800-531-8181	3,000	250	0.38%
Vanguard Money Market* (prime portfolio) www.vanguard.com 800-662-7447	3,000	250	0.33%

*I serve on the board of directors of this fund.

These money funds invest in large bank certificates, commercial paper (short-term corporate IOUs), government securities, and other instruments. Their yield, therefore, fluctuates fairly closely to the yields on these other instruments. To date, these yields have typically outpaced the interest offered on typical bank savings accounts. Because they pool the funds of many small investors, the money funds can buy large issues that are beyond the reach of individual investors. The funds sell for a dollar a share and have been able to keep the investor's principal constant. Any of the funds listed here would provide an excellent vehicle for an individual's cash reserves.

Bank Certificates of Deposit (CDs)

I have mentioned that a reserve for any known future expenditure should be invested in a safe instrument whose maturity matches the date on which the funds will be needed. Suppose, for example, you have set aside money for junior's tuition bills that will need to be paid at the end of one, two, and three years. One appropriate investment plan in this case would be to buy three bank CDs with maturities of one, two, and three years. Bank CDs are even safer than money funds, typically offer higher yields, and are an excellent medium for investors who can tie up their liquid funds for at least six months. Though the certificates are widely advertised as being government-insured up to $100,000 per buyer, that sum does not include any interest earnings that would bring the sum above $100,000. To be on the ultra safe side, you may not want to put more than $90,000 in the CDs from any single bank.

Bank CDs do have some disadvantages. They are not easily converted into cash. There is usually a penalty imposed for early withdrawal from your deposit. Also, the yield on CDs is subject to state and local income taxes. Treasury bills (short-term U.S. government IOUs), which are discussed below, are exempt from state and local taxes.

Bank CD rates vary widely. Today, with the nifty resources of the Internet, it's easy to find the most attractive returns. Just go to www.bankrate.com and search the site for the highest rates around the country. Deposits at all banks and credit unions listed at this site are reported to be insured by the Federal Deposit Insurance Corporation (FDIC). Addresses and phone numbers are given for each listing, and you can call to confirm that the deposits are insured and learn what current rates of return are being offered.

But remember that there's a price to be paid for obtaining a higher yield on a bank CD as opposed to a money-market fund: you have no check writing privileges, and you don't have ready access to your funds prior to maturity unless you pay a penalty.

INTERNET BANKS

Those comfortable with the wide, wide world of the Web might wish to take advantage of a new phenomenon: banks without walls. These are the on-line financial institutions that reduce their expenses by having neither branches nor tellers and by conducting all their business electronically. Because of their low overhead they can offer rates significantly above both typical savings accounts and money market funds. And, unlike money market funds, those Internet banks that are members of the FDIC can guarantee the safety of your funds.

How do you find an Internet bank? Go to the Google search engine and type in "Internet bank." You will also see the names of many popping up when you do a rate search on www.bankrate.com for the banks with the highest yields. Just make sure you see the words "member FDIC" before depositing any funds. The Internet banks generally post the highest CD rates available in the market.

TREASURY BILLS

Popularly known as T-bills, these are the safest financial instruments you can find and are widely treated as cash equivalents. Issued and guaranteed by the U.S. government to finance short-term needs, T-bills are auctioned with maturities of four weeks, three months, six months, or one year. They are sold at a minimum $1,000 face value and in $1,000 increments above that amount.

You can buy all but the four-week bills directly from the government, thus escaping transaction costs and commissions. T-bills offer an advantage over money-market funds and bank CDs in that their income is exempt from state and local taxes. In addition, T-bill yields are generally higher than those offered by money-market funds and typical bank savings accounts.

For further information on T-bills, check the government's Web site at www.publicdebt.treas.gov. For information on purchasing T-bills, go to www.treasurydirect.gov.

TAX-EXEMPT MONEY-MARKET FUNDS

If you find yourself lucky enough to be in the highest federal tax bracket, you will find tax-exempt money-market funds to be the best vehicle for your reserve funds. These funds invest in a portfolio of short-term, high-quality issues of state and local government entities and generate income that is exempt from federal taxes as well as from state taxes if the fund confines its investments to securities issued by entities within the state. As with regular money-market funds, they also offer free checking for amounts of $250 or more. The yields on these funds are lower than those of the taxable funds. Nevertheless, individuals in the highest income tax brackets will find the earnings from these funds more attractive than the after-tax yields on the regular money-market funds.

Most of the mutual fund complexes also offer state tax-exempt funds that only hold securities from your home state so that any earnings will be free of both federal and state taxes. If you live in a state with high state income taxes, these funds can be very attractive on an after-tax basis. You should call one of the mutual fund companies listed in the table below to find out if they have a money fund that only invests in the securities of the state in which you pay taxes.

Some Low-Expense Tax-Exempt Money-Market Funds

Fund Name	*Minimum Initial Purchase ($)*	*Minimum Amount for Check Withdrawal*	*Recent Expense Ratio (2002)*
Fidelity Municipal Money Market Fund www.fidelity.com 800-343-3548	$5,000	$500	0.43%
USAA Tax-Exempt Money Market Fund www.usaa.com 800-531-8181	3,000	250	0.48%
Vanguard Tax-Exempt Money Market Fund* www.vanguard.com 800-662-7447	3,000	250	0.18%

*I serve on the board of directors of this fund.

Buying Insurance

Most people need insurance. Those with family obligations are downright negligent if they don't purchase insurance. We risk death every time we get into our automobile or cross a busy street. A hurricane or fire could destroy our home and possessions. Most people are willing to pay some premium to protect themselves against the unpredictable.

Almost anything can be insured. Charles Whalen reports that the St. Louis Cardinals baseball team bought insurance during the 2000 season to protect against an injury to their current star at the time, Mark McGwire. The premise was that since McGwire regularly hit lots of home runs that translated into lots of tickets, ticket sales would fall if McGwire was injured. So the Cardinals bought an insurance policy that would pay the team if McGwire went on the disabled list. In such an event, the insurance company agreed to pay the Cardinals $20 for every empty seat below the team's average attendance.

For individuals, home and auto insurance are a must. So is health and disability insurance that is generally available from employers. Life insurance to protect one's family from the death of the breadwinner(s) is also a necessity. You don't need life insurance if you are single with no dependents. But if you have a family with young children who count on your income, you do need life insurance and lots of it.

There are two broad categories of life insurance products available: high-premium policies that combine insurance with an investment account, and low-premium term insurance that provides death benefits only, with no buildup of cash value.

The high-premium policies do have some advantages and are often touted for their tax-saving benefits. Earnings on the part of the insurance premiums that goes into the savings plan accumulate tax-free, and this can be advantageous for some individuals who have maxed out on their tax-deferred retirement savings plans. Moreover, individuals who will not save regularly may find that the periodic premium bills provide the discipline necessary for them to make sure that a certain amount will be available for their families if they die and that a cash value builds up on the investment part of the program. But policies of this kind provide the most advantages for the insurance agent who sells them and who collects high sales charges. Early premiums go mainly for sales commissions and other overhead rather than for buildup of cash value. Thus, not all your money goes to work. Hence, for most people, I favor the do-it-yourself approach. Buy term insurance for protection and invest the difference yourself in a tax-deferred retirement plan. The rules that follow will provide an investment plan that is far superior to that available from "whole life" or "variable life" insurance policies.

It's just common sense to buy term insurance, which provides substantial amounts of coverage for only relatively small premiums. There are, however, different kinds of term insurance. My advice is to buy renewable term insurance; you can keep renewing your policy without the need for a physical examination. So-called decreasing term insurance, renewable for progressively lower amounts, should suit many families best, because as time passes (and the children and family resources grow), the need for protection usually diminishes. You should understand, however, that term insurance premiums escalate sharply when you reach the age of sixty or seventy or higher. If you still need insurance at that point, you will find that term insurance has become prohibitively expensive. But the major risk at that point is not premature death; it is that you will live too long and outlive your assets. You can increase those assets more effectively by buying term insurance and putting the money you save into the investments I'll discuss in the rules that follow.

In 2003, states began adopting new mortality tables for insurers to use. Previously, insurance companies were using tables that were published in 1980. Since life expectancy has increased, insurance premiums have now fallen to reflect the decreased probability that insurers will be required to pay off the face value of the policy early. The longer people live, the less they need to pay for insurance.

One-year renewable term insurance policies will guarantee you coverage up to age seventy-five in most policies regardless of your health, but premiums will increase each year. Alternatively, you could purchase a level-premium term policy that fixes your premiums for a period of ten to thirty years. In the early years you will pay more for the level-premium policies, but the premiums will be less in the later years. If you think you will continue to need coverage over a substantial time period, the level-premium policies will usually be cheaper over the whole period of coverage.

Take the time to shop around for the best deal. There is considerable variation in insurance company rates. It is wise to use either telephone quote services or the Internet to ensure that you are getting the best deal. For example, you can go to www.term4sale.com. Enter your ZIP code, and you will be able to see a number of alternative policies at varying prices. There is no need to use an insurance agent. Policies available from agents will be more expensive since they need to include extra premiums to pay the agent's sales commission. Why pay a commission when you can get a much better deal by doing it yourself?

I recommend that you do not buy insurance from any company with an A. M. Best rating of less than A. A lower premium will not compensate you for taking any risk that your insurance company will get into financial difficulty and be unable to pay its claims. Don't bet your life on a poorly capitalized insurance carrier.

You can obtain A. M. Best's ratings of insurance companies by calling 908-439-2200. Insurance companies pay Best for the ratings. A somewhat more objective and critical rating is offered by Weiss Research, a consumer-supported company, which can be contacted at 800-289-9222.

Variable Annuities

An insurance product known as a variable annuity has recently been receiving a lot of press. I would avoid buying variable annuity products, especially the high-cost products offered by insurance salespeople. A variable annuity is essentially an investment product (typically a mutual fund) with an insurance feature. The insurance feature stipulates that if you die and the value of the investment fund has fallen below the amount you put in, the insurance company will pay back your full investment. These policies are very expensive because you typically pay high sales commissions and a premium for the insurance feature. Unless your mutual fund declines sharply with a fall in the stock market and you drop dead soon after purchasing a variable annuity, the value of this insurance is likely to be small. Remember the overarching rule for achieving financial security: Keep it simple. Avoid any complex financial products as well as the hungry agents who try to sell them to you. The only reason you should even consider a variable annuity is if you are super wealthy and have maxed out on all the other tax-deferred savings alternatives. And even then you should purchase such an annuity directly from one of the low-cost providers such as TIAA-CREF or the Vanguard Group.

RULE FOUR

Stiff the Tax Collector

One of the jokes traveling the rounds of the Internet goes as follows: A couple, both age seventy-eight, went to a sex therapist's office. The doctor asked, "What can I do for you?" The man said, "Will you watch us have sexual intercourse?" The doctor looked puzzled, but agreed. When the couple finished, the doctor said, "There's nothing wrong with the way you have intercourse," and charged them $50. The couple asked for another appointment and returned once a week for several weeks. They would have intercourse, pay the doctor, then leave. Finally, the doctor asked, "Just exactly what are you trying to find out?" The old man said, "We're not trying to find out anything. She's married and we can't go to her house. I'm married and we can't go to my house. The Holiday Inn charges $93 and the Hilton Inn charges $108. We do it here for $50, and I get $43 back from Medicare."

By telling this story, I do not mean to suggest that you attempt to cheat the government. But I do mean to suggest that you take advantage of every opportunity to make your savings tax-deductible and to let your savings and investments grow tax-free. The United States has a serious problem of inadequate saving: as a matter of national policy, a number of tax incentives have been enacted to encourage people to save. Millions of Americans are not taking advantage of these tax incentives. For most people, there is no reason to pay any taxes on the earnings from the investments that you make to provide for your retirement. Money can be sacked away in Individual Retirement Accounts and a variety of different kinds of pension plans. Almost all investors, except those who are super wealthy to begin with, can build up a substantial net worth in ways that ensure that nothing will be siphoned off by Uncle Sam. This rule tells you about the various tax incentives available and shows you how to leave the tax collector empty-handed.

Individual Retirement Accounts

Let's start with the simplest form of retirement plan, a straightforward Individual Retirement Account (IRA). You can take $3,000 per year and invest it in some investment vehicle such as a mutual fund and, for people with moderate income, deduct the entire $3,000 from taxes. (Individuals who earn relatively high incomes cannot take an initial tax deduction but they still get all the other tax advantages described below.) If you are in the 28 percent tax bracket, the contribution really costs you only $2,160, since the tax deduction saves you $840 in tax. You can think of it as having the government subsidize your savings account. Now suppose your investment earns 8 percent per year and you continue to put $3,000 per year into the account for forty-five years. No taxes whatsoever are paid on the earnings from funds deposited in an IRA. The investor who saves through an IRA has a final value of over $1.25 million, whereas the same contributions without the benefit of an IRA (where all the earnings are taxed at 28 percent each year) total only just over $450,000. Even after paying taxes at 28 percent on what you withdraw from the IRA (and in retirement you might even be in a lower tax bracket), you end up with close to $1 million. The chart below shows the dramatic advantage of investing through a tax-advantaged plan.

THE ADVANTAGE OF INVESTING THROUGH AN IRA
TAX-DEFERRED VS. TAXABLE INVESTING OF $3,000 A YEAR

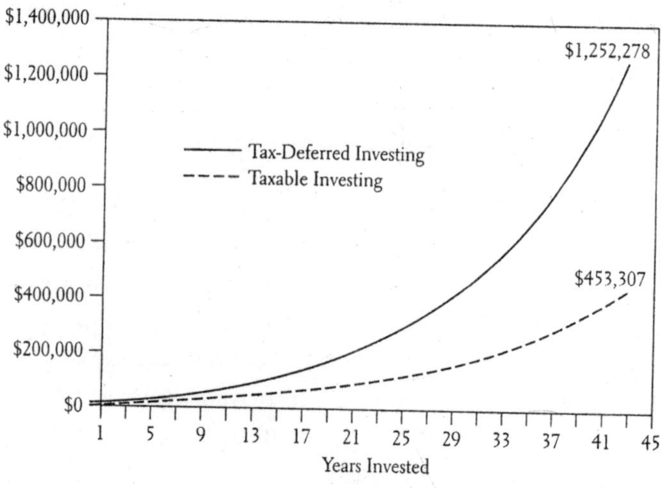

Source: John J. Brennan, *Straight Talk on Investing.*

This chart compares the final values of two hypothetical accounts, one tax-deferred and one taxable. In both accounts, the investors contributed $3,000 annually for 45 years and earned annual returns of 8 percent after expenses.

IRAs are also scheduled to get better over time. The contribution limit is scheduled to rise to $4,000 in 2005, and then rise again to $5,000 in 2008. Moreover, for those individuals who neglected to save early in life and who now must play catch-up, the limits are even higher, as shown in the table below.

Annual Contribution Limits for IRAs

Tax Year	*Under Age 50*	*Aged 50 or Over*
2003–04	$3,000	$3,500
2005	4,000	4,500
2006–07	4,000	5,000
2008 and later	5,000	6,000

Roth IRAs

During the late 1990s an additional form of individual retirement account called a Roth IRA became available to investors whose income is below certain levels. The traditional IRA offers "jam today" in the form of an immediate tax deduction (provided your income is low enough to make you eligible). Once in the account, the money and its earnings are only taxed when taken out at retirement. The Roth IRA offers "jam tomorrow"—you don't get an upfront tax deduction, but your withdrawals (including investment earnings) are completely tax-free. In addition, you can Roth and roll. You can roll your regular IRA into a Roth IRA if you are within certain income limits. You will need to pay tax on all the funds converted, but then neither future investment income nor withdrawals at retirement will be taxed. Moreover, there are no lifetime minimum distribution requirements for a Roth IRA and contributions can continue to be made after age seventy and a half. Thus significant amounts can be accumulated tax-free for the benefit of future generations.

The decision about which IRA is best for you and whether to convert can be a tough call. Important factors influencing the decision are whether you are likely to be in a higher or lower tax bracket at retirement, and whether you have sufficient funds outside your IRA to pay the conversion taxes. Other factors are your age and life expectancy. Fortunately, the financial services industry offers free software to analyze whether or not conversion makes sense for you. Many mutual fund companies and brokers have Roth analyzers that are reasonably easy to use. I can offer a rule of thumb to suggest whether further investigation is likely to be useful. If you are close to retirement and your tax bracket is likely to be lower in retirement, you probably shouldn't convert, especially if conversion will push you into a higher bracket now. On the other hand, if you are far from retirement and are in a lower tax bracket now, you are very likely to come out well ahead with a Roth IRA. If your income is too high to allow you to take a tax deduction on a regular IRA but low enough to qualify for a Roth, then there is no question that a Roth is right for you, since your contribution is made after tax in any event. But many baby boomers in their peak earnings years will have incomes too high to qualify for a Roth.

Pension Plans

A variety of pension plans are available from your employer. In addition, self-employed people can set up plans for themselves.

401(k) and 403(b) Pension Plans

Check if your employer has a pension profit-sharing plan such as a 401 (k), available from most corporate employers, or a 403(b), available from most educational institutions. These are perfect vehicles for saving and investing since the money gets taken out of your salary before you even see it. Moreover, many employers match some portion of the employee's contribution so that every dollar saved gets multiplied. As of 2003, as much as $12,000 per year can be contributed to these plans, and the contributions do not count as taxable income. For people over fifty, some of whom may need to play catch-up, contribution limits for 2003 are $14,000 per year. These contribution limits are scheduled to rise over time, as is shown in the table below.

Annual Limits for 401(k) and 403(b) Retirement Plans

Tax Year	*Under Age 50*	*Aged 50 or Over*
2003	$12,000	$14,000
2004	13,000	16,000
2005	14,000	18,000
2006 and later	15,000	20,000

Self-Employed Plans

For self-employed people, Congress has created the Keogh plan. All self-employed individuals—from accountants to Avon ladies, barbers to real estate brokers, doctors to decorators—are permitted to establish such a plan, to which they can contribute as much as 25 percent of their income, up to $30,000 annually. If you moonlight from your regular job, you can establish a Keogh for the income you earn on the side. The money paid into a Keogh is deductible from taxable income, and the earnings are not taxed until they are withdrawn. The plan is self-directed, which means the choice of how to invest is up to you. Any of the mutual fund companies that I will list in Rule 9 can do all the necessary paperwork for you.

A similar self-directed plan that is even easier to get up is a SEP-IRA. Contribution limits for the SEP are somewhat lower, however, as payments into the plan are capped at 15 percent of net income. If you qualify for either plan, you'll be making a big mistake not to take advantage of this perfectly legal way to checkmate the Internal Revenue Service and maximize your retirement savings.

Millions of taxpayers are currently missing what is one of the truly good deals around. My advice is to save as much as you can through these tax-sheltered means. Use up any other savings you may have for current living expenses, if you must, so you can contribute the maximum allowed.

What Can You Invest In?

What can retirement funds be invested in? You name it—stocks, bonds, mutual funds, savings certificates, and other investments. We will discuss how to allocate your funds in Rule 5. You can choose from a wide variety of plans offered by savings institutions, securities dealers, insurance companies, and mutual funds. My own preference would be stock and bond funds, and I'll give you specific advice for choosing the best vehicles in Rule 9. You certainly don't want to invest in lower-yield tax-exempt securities, however, because your retirement fund will accumulate tax-free anyway, and when you take the money out, you will pay taxes on what should have been tax-free income.

Any further questions regarding the plans? You can call your local office of the Internal Revenue Service for answers to specific questions. Also, IRS publications 590 (IRAs) and 560 (Keoghs) cover all the detailed regulations.

Priorities in Saving for Retirement

My recommendation is that you use every available vehicle to build up your wealth and ensure that you enjoy a retirement that is free from worry about money. But not everyone will be willing or able to make the sacrifices required to take advantage of all the opportunities available. The following list gives a set of priorities to guide you.

- First: Contribute to your employer 401(k) or 403(b) plan (or whatever new plan is available) up to the limit for employer matching contributions. If, for example, your employer will match your contribution dollar for dollar up to $3,000, then each dollar you contribute up to the limit will put $2 into your investment fund. And once you see that your taxes have been reduced by contributing up to the maximum limit set by the government, you'll be pleasantly surprised. You are missing a huge bonus if you don't take advantage of your employer's match.
- Second: Contribute to your employer plan, or an IRA, or your self-employment Keogh plan, or other available tax-advantaged retirement plan from your

employer up to the maximum contribution limit set by the government that will be tax-deductible.

- Third: Fund your IRA. Even if it is not tax-deductible, any earnings will accumulate tax-deferred, and everyone who can should make contributions up to the limit allowed.
- Fourth: Once you have maxed out on all other tax-advantaged opportunities, you could consider a variable annuity contract, which does have the advantage of tax deferral. As I indicated in Rule 3, however, these instruments involve very high fees, and while they may allow you to stiff the tax collector, they can also end up shortchanging you. Use only low-expense products that you can buy direct without sales charges, and buy them only after you have exhausted all other tax-saving opportunities.
- Fifth: Buy tax-exempt bonds issued by entities within your state and buy common stocks through the tax-efficient index funds suggested in rules 8 and 9.

The last point needs a bit of elaboration. Most people don't realize how tax-inefficient most mutual funds have become. Because the funds do lots of trading, often turning over their portfolios at least once a year, they tend to produce returns that are fully taxable. Two economists, John Shoven and Joel Dixon, examined the performance of sixty-two mutual funds over a thirty-year period from the 1960s through the 1990s. They found that a dollar invested in the typical fund would have grown to $21.89 in a tax-deferred account. But if the fund was held in a taxable account of a high-bracket investor, the dollar would have grown after tax to only $9.87. Taxes cut the net return by almost 60 percent. The point is that to the extent you do any investing outside a tax-advantaged retirement, you need to be very careful not to give away most of your hard-earned returns to the tax collector. The most tax-efficient equity funds available are those that simply buy and hold all the stocks in the market. Lists of these funds will be found in Rule 9.

A Caveat

One potential disadvantage of many of the tax-advantaged retirement plans is that you can't take the money out before you turn fifty-nine and a half, or unless you become disabled. If you do so, you will be taxed on the amount withdrawn and you will be required to pay an additional 10 percent penalty on it. Thus, you have to keep the funds invested and not touch them in order to gain the advantages. But perhaps this is really an advantage of our tax system since it encourages us to become long-term investors. Occasionally, lawmakers may actually do us a favor.

Possible New Tax-Favored Vehicles

As this book goes to press, President George W. Bush has proposed even larger limits for the tax-advantaged retirement plans. Moreover, he has proposed that the numerous current plans be collapsed into two basic ones in order to simplify the savings options available. The proposal would allow each individual to contribute up to $7,500 from earnings (so couples could contribute up to $15,000) into a Retirement Savings Account (RSA), which would replace current Roth IRAs. A second proposed vehicle called the Lifetime Savings Account would be even more alluring.

Each individual in a family could contribute $7,500 from any source. Thus, a family of four could contribute up to $45,000 per year into tax-advantaged savings plans ($15,000 from the Retirement Savings Account and $30,000 from the Lifetime Savings Account). The plans would work like Roth IRAs in that there would be no tax deduction for contributions made to the new plans. Current traditional IRAs could be rolled into the new RSAs but income taxes would have to be paid on conversion. But any earnings from the plans' investments—be they dividends, interest, or capital gains—would accumulate tax-free. And there would be no tax at all on any withdrawals from the plans. Such plans would eliminate all taxes on investments for virtually all investors but the super rich.

Want to know where things stand when you are ready to start a tax-advantaged savings for retirement program? Just call any of the 800 numbers of the mutual fund companies listed in Rule 9. Knowledgeable representatives will be able to answer your questions.

Tax-Free Savings Strategies for Education

These are also education savings plans. These plans have sometimes been described as "a license to steal" and, in a way, they are. But since the federal government sanctions them, you might as well take advantage.

Saving for College: As Easy as 529

"529" college savings accounts allow parents and grandparents to give gifts to children that can later be used for college education. Named after the provision of the tax code that sanctioned them, the gifts can be invested in stocks and bonds and no federal taxes will be imposed on the investment earnings as long as the withdrawals are made for qualified higher education purposes. The "kicker" is that qualifications are quite liberal. Does junior need a place to live while in college? Buy him an apartment! Does your darling daughter need transportation to class? Buy her the car of her dreams. As of 2003, the plans allowed an individual donor to contribute as much as $55,000 to a 529 plan without gift taxes and without reducing estate tax credits. For couples, the amount doubles to $110,000. Throw in four well-off and generous grandparents and there is $330,000 growing tax-free. If you have kids or grandchildren who plan to go to college and you can afford to contribute to a 529 plan, the decision to establish such a plan could well be a no-brainer.

Are there pitfalls to avoid? You bet. Most of the salespeople pushing these plans receive hefty commissions that eat into investment returns. Be an educated consumer and contact a company such as TIAA-CREF, Fidelity, or Vanguard for a no-load low-expense alternative. Also note that these 529 plans are sanctioned by individual states and some states allow you to take a tax deduction on your state income tax return for at least part if not all of your contribution. Thus, if you live in New York State (which allows a $5,000 per person deduction), you will want to be sure to get a New York plan. On the other hand, Massachusetts does not allow a state tax deduction for its own 529 plan, so residents can join a different state's plan. Moreover, if you don't use the proceeds of 529 plans for qualified education expenses (including midcareer retooling or even post-retirement education), withdrawals are not only subject to income tax but carry a 10 percent penalty as well.

Also, keep in mind that colleges are likely to consider 529 assets in determining need-based financial aid. In calculating eligibility for financial aid, many (if not most) colleges consider assets that are in the student's name more readily available for the payment of tuition than are assets in their parents' names. Thus, if you believe that your child will be eligible for financial aid, you and your spouse could be better off keeping the assets in your own names instead of investing in a 529 plan for your child. Of course, if you won't qualify for need-based aid in any case, by all means establish a low-expense 529. Comprehensive information about 529 plans, as well as other tax-advantaged savings vehicles such as ESAs, discussed below, can be found at www.savingforcollege.com.

Finally, if you are establishing a 529 for a teenager who will be going to college in a few years, you will probably want to weight your investments toward short-term bonds or bank certificates of deposit. Never invest money in the stock market that you will need in a short period of time.

Education Savings Accounts

Another tax-advantaged vehicle is the Education Savings Account (known as an ESA). Folks with moderate incomes may make contributions up to $2,000 per year on behalf of children under the age of eighteen. The funds can be withdrawn tax-free to meet legitimate education expenses. Obviously, you won't accumulate enough for four years of college under this plan, but it can help. But remember—colleges will consider amounts put aside in an ESA in figuring out financial aid.

Education Savings Bonds

Lastly, you should be aware of the government education savings bond program. Introduced by the U.S. Treasury in 1990, this program is available only to people with relatively low incomes. The EE and I government bonds that are used as investments can be bought directly from the government with no sales charge. As with 529 plans, any moneys earned on the bonds are tax-free when used for certain education expenses. There are somewhat stricter spending requirements than for 529 plans, however, as apartments, cars, and even books do not count as qualified expenditures. Check the government's Web site at www.publicdebt.treas.gov for further information.

The Best Tax Strategy of All

Probably the best thing you can do to reduce your tax burden is to buy your own home rather than renting. You have to live somewhere, and buying has several tax advantages over renting. Because Congress wanted to encourage home ownership and the social values associated with it, it gave the homeowner two important tax breaks. (1) Although rent is not deductible from income taxes, the two major expenses associated with home ownership—interest payments on your mortgage and property taxes—are fully deductible; and (2) realized gains in the value of your house up to $500,000 (joint filers) are tax-exempt. In addition, ownership of a house is a good way to force yourself to save, and a house provides enormous emotional satisfaction. My advice is: Own your own home if you can possibly afford it.

The family home has also proved to be a good investment. Remember Scarlett O'Hara? She was broke at the end of the Civil War, but she still had her beloved plantation, Tara. A good house on good land keeps its value no matter what happens to money. As long as the world's population continues to grow, the demand for real estate will be among the most dependable inflation hedges available.

How do you know if you can afford a home? The general rule of thumb is that a family should not spend more than 30 percent of its income on mortgage payments. With long-term fixed-rate mortgages below 6 percent at the time this book is being written, the pursuit of the American dream of your own home has never been easier. Every investing household should plan to own their own home.

RULE FIVE

Match Your Asset Mix to Your Investment Personality: How to Allocate Your Assets

ONCE YOU HAVE embarked on a steady, tax-advantaged savings program, the most important decision you need to make is how to allocate your assets among cash, bonds, common stocks, and real estate equities. Yogi Berra once offered the classic insight that "90 percent of success in baseball is mental." (Of course, he is best known for adding that the other 50 percent was physical.) Many studies have concluded that the major determinant (90 percent) of the overall rate of return earned by investors is not the particular bond or stock funds they buy, but rather the way they allocate their investment funds among the various asset classes. With this in mind, there are three factors that should determine the asset allocation that is right for you.

1. The time horizon over which you will be building up and holding your investments, a period that is likely

to be determined in significant part by your age.

2. Your financial circumstances, including the amount and stability of your non-investment income and your capacity to withstand investment reversals.
3. Your temperament, which determines your risk tolerance and the extent to which you are willing to accept the higher risks that are associated with higher returns.

It is important to emphasize that there is no universal, correct way to allocate your assets. Rather, you must match factors 1 and 2 to your own personality and temperament and then choose the asset mix that is appropriate for you.

A Reminder: Risk and Return Again

One of the principal tenets in the field of finance is that investment returns are related to the risk you are willing to assume. The higher the risk, the higher the return. The kicker in this equation is that measuring risk is well nigh impossible.

The *American Heritage Dictionary* defines "risk" as the possibility of suffering harm or loss. If I buy a six-month government-guaranteed bank CD to yield 4 percent and hold it to maturity, I am virtually certain of earning a 4 percent monetary return, before income taxes. The possibility of loss is so small as to be considered nonexistent. If I hold common stocks, however, hoping to earn their historical 10 percent average rate of return (including dividends and capital gains from the increase in their prices over time), I might be sorely disappointed. Indeed, during the period from March 2000 to October 2002, stocks of even the blue-chip companies making up the Dow Jones Industrial Average lost 40 percent of their value.

Financial professionals are still seeking the perfect way to measure risk. Risk here is defined as the chance of disappointment in achieving expected security returns. There is no way to associate a precise number with risk, but the pros have nevertheless come up with an arcane measure that defines risk as the probable variability or dispersion of future returns. This is a mouthful, and it supplies academics and obtuse members of the financial community with numerous opportunities to pontificate in words that no one understands. The end result is that risk now is generally defined as the typical variability of returns. In somewhat plainer English, risk is a measure of how much might be lost from investing in a particular asset class during unfavorable market periods.

The table below shows the average annual return as well as certain risk measures for three major asset classes (cash, bonds, and common stocks). Comparable long-run returns from real estate are not available but, in general, real estate has produced similar kinds of returns as have been available from common stocks as well as similar unruly tendencies.

Risk and Return 1926 Through 2002

	Average Annual Return	*Typical Volitility Range*	*Worst Return in a Single Year*
Cash (U.S. Treasury bills)	3½%	±3%	0
Bonds (U.S. Treasury)	5½%	±9%	−9%
Common stocks (large companies)	10%	±21%	−43%

Source: Ibbotson Associates.

Cash has been the most stable investment. Investors have never lost any dollar value from investing in Treasury bills but they have never made very much return either. Bonds have not been quite as stable. In the worst year, bonds lost 9 percent, and the typical range of returns including interest payments and changes in bond prices runs from plus 14 percent on the high end to minus 4 percent. Thus, bonds tend to swing in a range of plus or minus 9 percentage points around the 5½ percent average. But investors have on average earned a higher rate of return on bonds than from short-term bills as a compensation for their greater volatility.

Stocks are the wild cards, producing average returns far higher than Treasury bonds or short-term bills. But looking at the last column of the table, we see that in some years stocks get clobbered. In the worst year (during the Great Depression), stocks lost 43 percent in a single year. The middle column shows the typical range of returns that you might expect. By typical I mean that in two thirds of the years since 1926, returns have been contained within the ranges shown. Stock returns have behaved like a loose cannon, with returns typically ranging from plus 31 percent to minus 11 percent.

For a more dramatic look at the kinds of losses you must be prepared to accept if you buy common stocks, the next table shows the worst multi-year bear markets since the 1920s. The granddaddy of all bear markets ran from 1929 through 1932, when stocks fell 89 percent. The March 2000–October 2002 period was no picnic either, as large company stocks in the Dow Jones Industrial Average fell 40 percent. During that same period, the NASDAQ index of high-tech stocks declined by 78 percent. That is the reality of the risk you take by investing in the stock market.

Worst Stock Market Declines Since the Great Depression

(drop in the Dow Jones Industrial Average)

Period	*Percentage Decline*
1929–32	89%
1937–42	52%
1973–74	45%
2000–02	40%

There have been several five-year time periods when common stocks have actually produced consistently negative rates of return. The early 1930s were extremely poor for stock-market investors. The early 1970s also produced negative returns. The one-third decline in the broad stock-market averages during October 1987 is the most dramatic change in stock prices during a brief period since the 1930s. And stock investors know only too well how poorly stocks performed in the early years of the 2000s. Still, over the long haul, investors have been rewarded with higher returns for taking on more risk. Moreover, given the rate of return they seek, we will see that there are ways for investors to reduce the risks they take in investing in common stocks.

Your Time Horizon

It turns out that the longer you hold your stocks, the more you can reduce the risk you assume from investing in common stocks. The chart below makes the point convincingly. From 1950 through 2002, common stocks provided investors with an average annual return of a bit more than 10 percent. But in any single year the actual rate of return was either substantially above or below 10 percent. The single-year gains were as high as 53 percent; the single-year losses exceeded 25 percent. Clearly, if you are investing to meet some expenditure such as a college tuition payment next year, that money should not be put in common stocks because you have no assurance of earning a positive rate of return over such a short period.

RANGE OF ANNUAL RETURNS ON COMMON STOCKS FOR VARIOUS TIME PERIODS, 1950–2002

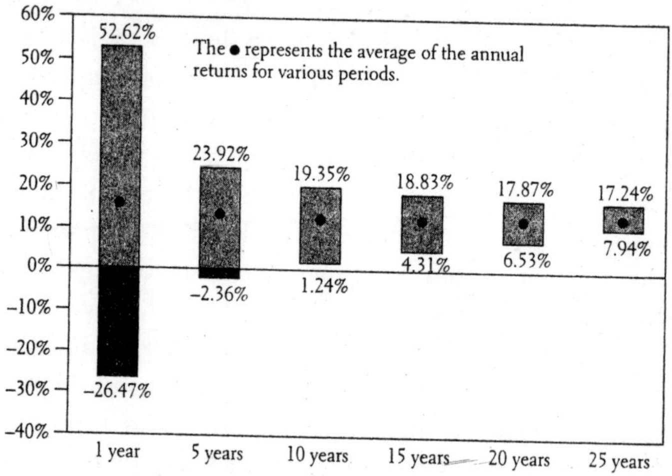

But note how the picture changes if you can put your money away for twenty-five years. The range of historical outcomes is much narrower. Indeed, even during the worst 25-year period you would have earned a rate of return of almost 8 percent—a quite generous return and one that was larger than the long-run average return from relatively safe bonds. This is why stocks are a wholly appropriate medium for investing in long-term retirement funds. I have prepared the next table, below, to indicate the *maximum* percentage of your assets that should be invested in stocks *based solely on your time horizon.* You can be relatively sure of earning a generous rate of return from stocks only if you hold them for a long period of time. When you hold stocks long enough, they become less risky. Note, however, that other considerations will most likely call for adjustments in the proportions suggested here.

Investment Period and Maximum Equity Exposure

Expected Period During which You Will Hold Your Investments	*Maximum Equity Exposure (%)*
1–5 years	0
5–10 years	33
10–20 years	66
20 years and longer	100

If no other consideration than your investment period mattered, this phenomenon of risk reduction over time would make your age an important determinant of the correct asset mix for you. If you are in your twenties or thirties and beginning an investment program for retirement, you can safely put most or all of your savings into common stocks because your holding period is likely to be more than twenty years. On the other hand, if you are already retired and expect to spend your accumulated savings over the relatively near term, only a moderate equity exposure is appropriate, and your portfolio should have substantial amounts of bonds that will provide more predictable returns.

One rule of thumb used by some investment advisers is to set the proportion of bonds in your portfolio equal to your age. A woman in her twenties should keep only 20 percent of her portfolio in relatively safe bonds and 80 percent in equities. A man aged seventy-five should put no more than 25 percent of his portfolio in stocks, and that equity exposure should probably contain a substantial proportion of real estate investment trusts with their generous dividend yields that can be used for living expenses. In Rule 9, I will suggest actual investments that you can use to make your asset allocation consistent with this principle.

There is one adjustment to the age rule of thumb just described. Many older people want to leave some of their wealth to their children or perhaps to some charitable foundation. In such a case, age is not an appropriate indicator of investment horizon. Such people can safely have more of their assets in equities provided they have the capacity for risk described below. Moreover, many older Americans with the right genes and with some exercise and healthy eating will be spending a lot more years in retirement than was the case for earlier generations. Further, always remember that equities are never an appropriate investment for funds put aside to meet some short-term financial commitment.

Your Capacity for Risk

Your appropriate asset allocation also depends on your capacity for risk. This is quite different from your attitude toward risk. Your attitude reflects your psychological comfort. Your capacity has to do with your financial survival. The kind of investments that are appropriate for your risk capacity depends upon your sources of income other than those derived from your investment portfolio. Often this capacity is related to your age and reinforces the suggestions made above. I like to use two illustrations to help you understand the concept.

Mildred G. is a recently widowed sixty-eight-year-old.

She has been forced to give up her job as a registered nurse because of her increasingly severe arthritis. Her modest house in Homewood, Illinois, is still mortgaged. While this fixed-rate home mortgage was taken out some time ago at a relatively low rate, it does involve a substantial monthly payment. Apart from monthly Social Security payments, all Mildred has to live on are the earnings on a $250,000 group insurance policy on which she is the beneficiary and a $50,000 portfolio of small growth stocks that had been accumulated over a long number of years by her late husband.

It is clear that Mildred's capacity to bear risk is severely constrained by her financial situation. She has neither a long life expectancy nor the physical ability to earn income outside her portfolio. Moreover, she has substantial fixed expenditures on her mortgage. She would have no ability to recoup a loss on her portfolio. A portfolio weighted toward safe bonds that can generate substantial income is what is appropriate for Mildred. Risky stocks of small growth companies—no matter how attractive their prices may be—do not belong in her portfolio. Whatever equities she owns should be weighted toward real estate equities that provide generous dividend yields.

Tiffany B., an ambitious, single twenty-six-year-old with a new MBA from the Graduate School of Business at Stanford, has entered a training program that will lead to a position as a loan officer at San Francisco's Wells Fargo Bank. She has just inherited a $50,000 legacy from her grandmother's estate. Her goal is to build a sizable portfolio, which in later years could finance the purchase of a home and be available as a retirement nest egg.

For Tiffany, one can safely recommend an "aggressive

young businesswoman's" portfolio. She has both a long life expectancy and the earning power to maintain her standard of living in the face of any financial loss. While her personality will determine the precise amount of risk exposure she is willing to undertake, it is clear that Tiffany's portfolio belongs toward the far end of the risk-reward spectrum. Tiffany has both the investment horizon and the capacity to assume risk that allows her to have a 100 percent equity portfolio.

Your Temperament

By far the most important adjustment to the general asset allocation guidelines suggested above concerns matching the mix of assets you choose to your attitude toward risk. The key question is what asset allocation allows you to sleep at night. If you choose to start a program of investing in common stocks, it is crucial that you have the temperament to stick with it, even when everyone is pessimistic. Above all, you must be able to resist the temptation to sell your stocks after they have just declined sharply in value. You may have all of the right qualifications to allocate your portfolio largely to equities. You may be young and have a good steady income from employment. But if you are emotionally unable to accept the roller-coaster ride that is invariably associated with investing in common stocks, then a substantial exposure to equities is not for you.

No finance professor, church pastor, or psychiatrist can tell you what your risk tolerance ought to be. Risk tolerance is an essential aspect of any financial plan, and only you can evaluate your attitude toward risk. You can take some comfort in knowing that risk is reduced by investing regular amounts over time, and it is also reduced if you have a long investment horizon. But if you invest in common stocks, you must have the temperament to accept their considerable volatility. If you were an investor during the early 2000s, you know that the stock market declined quarter after quarter. How did you feel when the Dow Jones Industrial Average dropped from 10,000 in mid-June to 7,200 in early October of 2002? If you panicked and became physically ill because a large portion of your assets was invested in common stocks, then clearly you need to pare down the equity portion of your investment program. Thus, subjective considerations must play an important role in determining the asset mix that is right for you.

J. P. Morgan once had a friend who was so worried about his stock holdings that he could not sleep at night. The friend asked, "What should I do about my stocks?" Morgan replied, "Sell down to the sleeping point." He wasn't kidding. Every investor must decide the trade-off he or she is willing to make between eating well and sleeping well. The decision is up to you. High investment rewards can be achieved only at the cost of substantial risk-taking. This has been one of the fundamental lessons of this book. So what's your sleeping point? Finding the answer to this question is one of the most important investment steps you must take.

In his book *Rational Investing in Irrational Times*, Larry Swedroe suggests that you take the following test: Assume you have $100,000 to invest and decide what percent of that stake you could afford to lose without panicking or losing sleep. Suppose it is $20,000 or 20 percent of your investment. Then go to the table below and figure out your maximum exposure to common stocks.

Ability to Withstand Loss and Maximum Equity Exposure

Maximum Tolerable Loss (%)	*Maximum Exposure to Common Stocks (%)*
5	20
10	30
15	40
20	50
25	60
30	70
35	80
40	90
50	100

These percentages may or may not work for everyone, but it's clear that one's emotional makeup, particularly during periods of market stress, must play an important role in the asset allocation that is right for you.

Rebalancing, or Keeping an Even Temperament

Suppose you are quite risk averse and follow a very conservative asset allocation rule—half stocks and half bonds. Even if you are in your early thirties, this is the right allocation for your temperament. You therefore put half of your regular savings into an equity fund and half into a bond fund. Movements in the bond and stock markets will tend to shift your allocation over time. Small changes (plus or minus 10 or even 15 percent) should probably be ignored. But what if the stock market doubles in a short period of time and bond values stay constant? All of a sudden you will find that two thirds of your assets are in stocks and one third are in bonds. Or what if the stock market falls sharply and bonds rise in price, as was the experience of investors in 2002? What do you do then?

The correct response is to make small changes in the mix of your portfolio. This is known as "rebalancing," and it involves not letting the asset proportions in your portfolio stray too far from the ideal mix you have chosen. For example, if the equity portion is too high, you could put all new allocations, as well as the dividends paid from your equity investments, into bond investments. If the balance is severely out of whack, you can shift some of your money from the equity to the bond fund. Alternatively, if the bond portion has increased over your desired allocation, you can move money into the equity fund. The correct response to a fall in the price of one asset class is not to panic and sell out. Rather, you need the discipline and fortitude to buy more. Sharp market declines will make rebalancing seem like a frustrating way to lose even more money. But in the long run, investors who have rebalanced their portfolios in a disciplined way have been generously rewarded. Don't be trigger-happy. But rebalance at least once a year.

You also may well want to consider rebalancing as you age. For most people, a safer asset mix that has a somewhat reduced equity mix will make for a less stressful retirement. In Rule 9, I will suggest actual investments consistent with the asset allocation principles outlined here.

RULE SIX

Never Forget That Diversity Reduces Adversity

ALAS, there's nothing new about this rule. Four hundred years ago, in his epic novel *Don Quixote,* Cervantes advised that one should not "venture all his eggs in one basket." But just as Don Quixote was regarded as a silly buffoon in his travels, so too has been the pithy advice of Cervantes, particularly during recent times when thousands of people sunk, literally sunk, all their assets in high-tech stocks.

It is important to recognize, however, that diversification is in a sense a two-edged sword. You need not only to hold different major asset categories (cash, bonds, stocks, and real estate) but also to diversify your holdings within each category.

This advice, too, is not all that new.

THE BENEFITS OF DIVERSIFICATION

William Sharpe, a Nobel Prize–winning financial economist, provides this simple example of the benefits of the oldest investment rule in the book, always diversify your investments to reduce risk.

> At one time, each ship sent from London to bring back spices from the Orient was financed by one merchant. If the ship happened to sink, the investor lost everything. But if several merchants pooled their resources, with each taking partial interests in several ships, risk could be greatly reduced, with no diminution in overall expected return. Such pooling could be accomplished in a number of ways. One of the simpler procedures involved the issuance of "ownership shares" (not surprisingly), with each investor holding a *diversified portfolio* of shares in several ships.

Similarly for investors, the correct investment strategy is to diversify your security holdings within an investment category and to hold a variety of different asset categories.

Cash investments do not usually need to be diversified. If you check your money-market fund holdings, you will find that the fund holds a wide variety of short-term securities issued by government, banks, and high-quality corporations. If you have money in Treasury bills or in an insured bank CD, you also need not worry about diversification. You need to diversify your bank CD holdings only to the extent that you have no more than $100,000 in any FDIC institution.

Bonds, the darlings of the investment world in the three years from 2000 through 2002, are another matter. While high-quality bonds, such as U.S. government bonds, rallied in price as interest rates fell, money invested in the bonds of WorldCom fell even faster than many stock prices. By itself, bond is a four-letter word. Add that all-important plural "s" for diversity, and you'll find that bonds provide very important diversification advantages. Similarly, for real estate investment trusts, broad diversification is a necessity. A single REIT might own a diversified portfolio of office buildings in a single area of the country. If that region does poorly, so will your REIT. What is needed is a fund of REITs broadly diversified both by region and property type. Never, ever forget: diversity reduces adversity.

An Investment Horror Story

Stocks, of course, present the saddest and most horrific stories of what happens when holdings are not diversified.

Take the example of Charlotte Simmons (not her real name). She was a happy employee of the Enron Corporation. What could be better than to work for one of America's leading New Economy companies? Enron was at the cutting edge of the movement to revolutionize the markets for electric power and mass communications. Its chief executive officer, Kenneth Lay, was accorded the status of a rock star, and business publications praised him as a mastermind. In the competitive and growing markets for power and communications, Enron was in the best position to profit by arranging trades of fiber-optic capacity and power from those who had a surplus to those who needed it. The company's stock was the darling of the Wall Street community, with almost twenty of the leading investment firms rating it a "strong buy." Security analysts and Enron executives regularly appeared on CNBC to give glowing reports about the company's prospects. Enron was likened to the young Elvis Presley crashing onto the scene and revolutionizing popular music. The old power companies were like old fogies dancing to the records of Guy Lombardo. Enron doubled and then doubled again. The sky was the limit.

Charlotte was also fortunate because she had a 401(k) retirement plan. One of the investment options in the plan was to purchase Enron common stock. The company itself matched employee contributions up to some limit, with the match paid in Enron stock. Following the advice of the charismatic leaders of the company, Charlotte decided to put all of her contributions into Enron stock as well. And how proud she was that she had done so. She was fifty-eight years old, had never made more than a very modest salary, but because she had the "genius" to roll the dice and put everything into Enron, she now had a retirement kitty worth $2.5 million. She made her plans to retire in two years at the age of sixty and looked forward to a comfortable life of leisure and world travel.

You know the sad end of the story. It turned out that the success of Enron was built on a mosaic of fraudulent trading schemes and phony accounting. The company collapsed and the stock became worthless. Charlotte did get her wish for more leisure: she was fired from the company. Her $2.5 million retirement kitty simply vaporized. She had lost not only her job but all of her money. Not only did she fail to diversify her investment portfolio, but she also put herself in jeopardy by subjecting her income from employment to the same risks as her investments. Charlotte failed to heed Rule 6: Diversity Reduces Adversity.

The Potential Crises in Some 401(k) Plans

The Enron saga is not an isolated example. WorldCom went belly up after it was revealed that fraudulent accounting had hidden $7 billion of expenses from its financial reports. Fully 40 percent of the employee assets in the company's 401(k) retirement plan were invested in WorldCom stock—now essentially worthless. A substantial proportion of the U.S. companies in the Standard & Poor's 500-Stock Index have at least half of their 401(k) assets invested in their own stock. There is a dangerous concentration in America's corporate retirement plans. This represents a potential crisis of untold magnitude.

I understand the implicit pressure that is often put on employees to hold a substantial share of their retirement fund in the company's stock. It is often considered a sign of loyalty. And I also understand that employees of companies such as Microsoft were very happy to concentrate their retirement savings in one single stock. But for every Microsoft there was at least one WorldCom. *Never* put a single dollar in your retirement plan over and above the amount of company stock you are required to hold because of the company's matching retirement savings policy. Workers should not bear the enormous level of risk involved when one's livelihood as well as one's retirement fund depends on the prospects of one company, no matter how good that company may appear.

How Much Diversification Is Enough?

Investing in a broad portfolio of stocks is a far less risky proposition than putting all of your eggs in one basket—particularly if the one basket in question is a stock like Enron or WorldCom. Perhaps a coin-flipping example will help make the point. Suppose a $100 stock has a 50-50 chance of either moving up to $220 (for a 120 percent return) or falling to zero (saddling the investor with a 100 percent loss). We can think of the situation as gamble of $100 based on the toss of a fair coin. If the coin comes up heads, you get $220; if tails, you get 0. In probabilistic terms, the gamble gives you a 10 percent return. You have a 50 percent probability of making $120 and a 50 percent probability of losing the whole $100.* This looks like a reasonable deal since the odds are in your favor, but with an unfavorable flip you lose your whole investment—an unacceptable risk.

Now suppose there are ten different stocks—all offering the same odds and same payoffs—and you invest $1,000, $100 in each. Ten different fair coins will be tossed; in each case a head turns your $100 into $220, while a tail turns your $100 into dust. As long as one coin toss is independent of another, your risk is substantially reduced. On average, five tosses will be heads—producing gains of $600 ($120 gain × 5)—and five tosses will be tails (involving a loss of $500 [$100 loss × 5]). On average, you make $100 on your $1,000 investment—the same 10 percent expected return. But notice that your risk is substantially reduced. The only way you could lose your entire stake is to have all ten coin tosses come up tails (a highly unlikely event with a fair coin—try it yourself). Finally, suppose you buy into a fund that holds thousands of stocks. I think you can see that it would be virtually impossible for such an investment to go the way of Enron.

Basically, what happens when you buy a portfolio of many stocks is that you reduce your risk substantially. Some of your investments may fail: The pharmaceutical company's leading drug is found to cause cancer, the main

*The expected return is $\frac{1}{2}(120) + \frac{1}{2}(-100) = 10$ which is 10 percent of your initial stake.

plant of a chemical company blows up, the managers of another company are found to be raiding the assets and covering it up with phony accounting. Other companies will prove to be successful: Another pharmaceutical company discovers an important new drug, an oil company makes a significant oil discovery, and your Internet company becomes the leader in on-line auctions. By holding a wide variety of stocks, you reduce risk considerably because economic events don't affect all companies the same way, and unfavorable company-specific events are likely to be balanced by very favorable events for other companies.

How many stocks are enough to achieve adequate diversification? The answer is that it may take up to one hundred different stocks to reduce the riskiness of investing in stocks to prudently low levels. For individual investors who will be building up their retirement account over time, this necessitates that the vehicle you should choose is the equity mutual fund. The mutual fund pools the monies from hundreds of thousands of investors and purchases a (usually) diversified portfolio of stocks. The fund shareholder holds a pro rata share in all the securities that the fund holds. The fund does all the bookkeeping, distributes the dividends from the fund's investments, or reinvests them back into the fund as most retirement savers will desire. If you want to take some extra money and gamble it on some high-flying biotech stock, go ahead—it is likely to be at least as rewarding as going to the racetrack or Las Vegas. But for your serious retirement money, don't buy individual stocks—buy mutual funds. And in Rule 9, I will tell you the best, lowest-cost, and most diversified investment funds available.

Do You Need to Diversify Internationally?

Many analysts recommend that investments be diversified internationally as well as domestically. The argument is that economic activity in various parts of the world does not move in lockstep. We know, for example, that during the 1990s, when the U.S. economy was booming, Japan's economy was stagnating. And when stock returns were poor in the United States and Europe, during the early 2000s, the stocks of some emerging markets actually rose. In 2003, when the U.S. dollar was falling, European currencies were rising, giving an added boost to European stocks. So returns will tend to be more stable if a portfolio is diversified by including stocks from countries all over the world.

There is much to be said in favor of this argument, and for investors with substantial resources, I do recommend supplementing a broad-based U.S. stock index with one that invests in stocks from the world economies outside the United States. There is a broad-based, non-U.S., developed country index fund that tracks the EAFE index (an index of stocks from Europe, Australasia, and the Far East). An index that includes the stocks in the developing economies is the Morgan Stanley Capital International Emerging Markets Index, and funds exist that track that index. But for most people of modest means, I go back to my mantra: Keep it simple. You can get along fine by just investing in U.S. companies.

There are a number of reasons why investors of modest means need not diversify internationally. First, globalization has linked our world economies more and more closely over time. Economic activity throughout the world is much more closely correlated today than was the case decades ago. Worse, the correlations among nations are especially high during recessionary economic periods. It is often said that when the United States catches cold, the rest of the world gets pneumonia. Recessions get transmitted around the globe, and when the U.S. stock market goes into a tailspin, other markets now usually follow. Moreover, during periods of substantial geopolitical risk, all global stock markets tend to decline together. Thus, international diversification as a risk reducer, through offsetting variations in the economies of the rest of the world, tends to fail us just when we need it most. Finally, since most large U.S. corporations obtain a significant share of their revenues and profits from overseas operations, a portfolio of U.S. stocks is already internationally diversified to a significant extent.

Diversification Also Means Buying Other Asset Classes

Just as you need to hold a diversified portfolio of stocks to moderate your investment risk, so also you need to balance a stock portfolio with other asset classes. Your retirement portfolio should contain real estate securities as well as bonds. Both will tend to dampen the fluctuations in the dollar value of your portfolio and help you sleep better at night.

Let's consider bonds first. During the three years from 2000 through 2002, if your portfolio contained nothing but common stocks, you would not have been a happy camper. Even a broadly diversified fund holding equities declined over 40 percent in value. But during that same time period, bond prices rose smartly, and diversified bond portfolios provided quite generous returns. A portfolio diversified between a broad-based bond fund and stock fund exhibited a good deal more stability than one that included only equities. While the market was soaring in the late 1990s, many investors eschewed bonds as suitable only for old fogies. But bonds showed their diversification advantages very well early in the new millennium, just when you needed diversification the most.

There are also compelling reasons to diversify a portfolio with real estate equities. A broadly diversified REIT fund that holds individual REITs specializing in different regions and in different property types will provide attractive diversification benefits for investors. Real estate returns don't always move in lockstep with other assets. For example, during periods of accelerating inflation, properties tend to do much better than other common stocks. Thus, adding real estate to a portfolio tends to reduce its overall volatility. I'll make use of both bonds and real estate in the specific portfolios that I will recommend in Rule 9.

Another asset class that is frequently recommended for further diversification benefits is international stocks, including those from the emerging markets of the world. If you have substantial assets you may well want to hold an equity portfolio that is internationally as well as domestically diversified. Those with substantial assets could hold up to one quarter of their equity holdings in international stocks. For folks of modest means, however, I think you could keep life simple and just hold U.S. stocks for the reasons suggested above.

Diversification Over Time

Risk is also reduced for investors who build up a retirement nest egg by putting their money in the market regularly over time. If you had to make all your investments at a single time, you might have been unlucky enough to buy all your stocks in March 2000—just at the peak of the market. By building up their investment portfolio slowly over time, savers can be sure that some of their monies will be invested during very favorable periods when prices are low. Investment professionals call this technique "dollar-cost averaging."

Dollar-cost averaging simply means investing the same fixed amount of money in the shares of some mutual fund or other investment at regular intervals—say, every month or quarter—over a long period of time. Periodic investments of equal dollar amounts in common stocks can reduce (but not avoid) the risks of equity investment by ensuring that the entire portfolio of stocks will not be purchased at temporarily inflated prices. The investor who makes equal dollar investments will buy fewer shares when prices are high and more shares when prices are low. As the following table illustrates, the average cost per share is actually lower than the average of the share prices during the period when the investments are made.

In this example, I assume that you put $150 per period into a mutual fund whose share price fluctuates between $25 and $75. By the process of dollar-cost averaging, you have purchased eleven shares, now worth $50 apiece, for a total market value of $550, although you have invested only $450 over the period. In other words, your average share cost ($450/11 = $40.91) is lower than the average

($50) of the market price of the fund's shares during the periods in which they are accumulated. So you've actually made money despite the fact that the average price at which you bought is the same as the current price. It works because you bought more shares when they were cheap and fewer when they were dear.

Illustration of Dollar-Cost Averaging

Period	*Investment*	*Price of Fund Shares*	*Shares Purchased*
1	$150	$75	2
2	150	25	6
3	150	50	3
Total cost	$450		
Average price		$50	
Total shares owned			11

Value of shares earned $550
Average cost: approximately $41

With dollar-cost averaging, there are circumstances where you could actually come out better in a market where prices are very volatile and don't rise over time than you would if you were investing in an ebullient market environment. Consider the following two stock-market scenarios:

Two Different Market Scenarios

Period	*Volatile Market That Ends up Flat*	*Ebullient Market That Rises Continually*
1	$100	$100
2	80	110
3	60	120
4	80	130
5	100	140

Most people would think that their retirement assets would be much better off with a market that rose continuously. But suppose you invested $1,000 per period. The table below shows that you actually end up with more money in the scenario where the market is very volatile and ends up exactly where it began. In both cases, a total of $5,000 is invested over the five periods. In the flat volatile market, the investor ends up with $6,167, while in the scenario where market prices rise continually, the investor's final fund stake is only $5,915.

THE BENEFITS OF DOLLAR-COST AVERAGING

	VOLATILE MARKET THAT ENDS UP FLAT			EBULLIENT MARKET THAT RISES CONTINUALLY		
Period	*Amount Invested*	*Price of Index*	*Number of Shares Purchased*	*Amount Invested*	*Price of Index*	*Number of Shares Purchased*
1	$1,000	$100	10	$1,000	$100	10
2	1,000	80	12.5	1,000	110	9.09
3	1,000	60	16.67	1,000	120	8.33
4	1,000	80	12.5	1,000	130	7.69
5	1,000	100	10	1,000	140	7.14
Amount invested	$5,000			$5,000		
Total shares purchased			61.67			42.25
Average cost of shares purchased		$81.08			$118.34	
Value at period 5		$6,167			$5,915	

Warren Buffett, one of the world's truly legendary investors, has a very nice way of showing that you might actually wish for lower stock prices (at least for awhile) after you begin your investment program. In one of his essays, Buffett writes:

A short quiz: If you plan to eat hamburgers throughout your life and are not a cattle producer, should you wish for higher or lower prices for beef? Likewise, if you are going to buy a car from time to time but are not an auto manufacturer, should you prefer higher or lower car prices? These questions, of course, answer themselves.

But now for the final exam: If you expect to be a net saver during the next five years, should you hope for a higher or lower stock market during that period? Many investors get this one wrong. Even though they are going to be net buyers of stocks for many years to come, they are elated when stock prices rise and depressed when they fall. In effect, they rejoice because prices have risen for the "hamburgers" they will soon be buying. This reaction makes no sense. Only those who will be sellers of equities in the near future should be happy at seeing stocks rise. Prospective purchasers should much prefer sinking prices.

Don't think that dollar-cost averaging will solve all of your investment problems. No plan can protect you against a loss in market value during declining stock markets. And a critical feature of the plan is that you have both the cash and the courage to continue to invest during bear markets as regularly as you do in better periods. No matter how pessimistic you are (and everybody else is), and no matter how bad the financial and world news is, you must not interrupt the automatic pilot nature of the plan or you will lose the important benefit of ensuring that you buy at least some of your shares after a sharp market decline. Indeed, if you can buy a few extra shares whenever the market declines by 20 to 25 percent, your dollar-cost averaging will work even better. The worst thing you could do is to sell out after the market declines.

I'm not suggesting for a minute that you try to forecast the market. No one can do that. However, it's usually a good time to buy after the market has fallen out of bed and no one can think of any reason why it should rise. Just as hope and greed can sometimes feed on themselves to produce speculative bubbles, so do pessimism and despair react to produce market panics. The greatest market panics are just as unfounded as the most pathological speculative explosions. No matter how bleak the outlook has been in the past, things usually got better. For the stock market as a whole, Newton's law has always worked in reverse: What goes down has always gone back up.

RULE SEVEN

Pay Yourself, Not the Piper

IMAGINE SOMEONE telling you: "Invest with me, and when you are ready to retire, I'll take half your retirement nest egg as my fee." Financial firms won't tell you that, but that's what many do. Whether you buy insurance products, mutual funds, or even if you buy individual stocks directly, the sales charges and ongoing expenses you pay will make a dramatic difference in the cumulative value of your portfolio. In horse racing, the horse carrying the lightest jockey has a substantial advantage. The situation is no different over the long run in the investment race. Suppose, for example, you invest $1,000 for forty years in a low-expense mutual fund returning 8 percent after all costs. In forty years, your $1,000 will have grown to $21,725. Now imagine that you invested in a fund holding the same assets, but that annual expenses were an extra 2 percentage points per year, so that the net return to you was only 6 percent.

In this case, your $1,000 would grow in forty years to only $10,286. What I've shown is that an extra 2 percentage points of expense cuts your final stake by more than half—losing you more than $10,000 that could make your retirement more comfortable. Costs, however, are an important consideration for all financial products and services, starting with the ubiquitous credit card.

Pay Off All Credit Card Bills

As I recommended earlier, the first step in paying yourself rather than someone else involves your credit card(s). Probably the biggest cost that can wreak havoc with your financial future is to allow yourself to get saddled with credit card debt. There is no way you can get ahead of the game if you are paying 18 percent a year interest on your credit card. Soon, your monthly payments will barely be able to keep up with your interest payments, and your balance of indebtedness will never go down. There are few "never" rules in personal finance, but the one that I recommend is: Never allow yourself to build up credit card debt. And if you do have credit card debt, your first steps to financial security should be to get rid of that debt as soon as possible.

If you own a home and have credit card debt, take out a low-cost home equity loan and pay off the debt. Interest on the home equity loan is likely to be tax-deductible as well. If you have no other resources, use the tricks I suggested in Rule 2 to rein in your weekly expenditures. Despite all my admonitions to start a tax-advantaged savings plan now, you should not do so while you have high-interest credit card debt outstanding. The safest thing you can do to start on the road to financial security is to put every dollar of saving into credit card debt repayment. It's like investing in a perfectly safe 18 percent bond—no other investment exists that can provide that large a risk-free return. Paying off credit card debt is the best investment you will ever make.

Look Out for Mutual Fund Expenses

We have seen that the magic of compounding turns into the tyranny of compounding as the effects of higher costs keep dragging down the value of your portfolio each year. And let me assure you, many financial services companies make every effort to obscure the total costs you are actually paying for their management services and for the sales costs they incur to obtain new clients, such as their advertising budget.

Costs play a crucial—indeed, I would say the crucial—role in shaping the long-run returns that investors actually receive from mutual funds. As Jack Bogle, the founder and former chairman of the Vanguard Group of Investment Companies, has written, "a low expense ratio is the major reason why a [mutual] fund does well. . . . The surest route to top-quartile returns is bottom-quartile expenses." The only factor reliably linked to future mutual fund performance is the expense ratio charged by the fund. But the direct management expenses are only a part of the problem. Most mutual funds turn over their entire portfolio once a year through purchases and sales of securities, adding as much as one additional percentage point in transactions costs to the management expenses they charge.

The first thing to look at when you are contemplating the purchase of any mutual fund is its expense ratio. A fund with an expense ratio of 20 basis points (20/100 of 1 percent) is fighting a 20-knot breeze in attempting to win the sailing race. A fund with a 150 basis point expense rate (1.5 percentage points per year) is, in the words of Jack Bogle, "fighting a 150 knot typhoon." In Rule 9, I will recommend a selection of funds that have low expense ratios.

Every extra dollar of expense you pay is skimmed from your investment capital. Those funds are lost forever. They will never be able to compound and grow over time. Over the long run, sales charges, loads, and higher expenses inevitably drag down your returns. *Never* buy a mutual fund with a load charge. *Never* buy a newly issued fund from a broker even if the broker tells you there is no commission. The fund pays the brokerage firm a large commission to sell the new shares, and you will be paying one dollar for about 94 cents of assets. In effect, you will be paying a large load fee even though your broker has assured you that your purchase was commission free. Over time, the costs you pay to your fund management company will make a dramatic difference in the final nest egg you can accumulate at retirement. The financial markets are like a gambling casino, but unlike a casino, the odds are in your favor. What you need to ensure is that the casino's "take" (the cost of playing the game) is as small as possible. Keep expenses to a minimum and thus keep investment returns in your pocket rather than in the pockets of the croupiers.

The situation is exactly the same for money-market funds and bond funds. Indeed, the gross variation in returns for money-market and bond funds tends to be very much smaller than is the case for equity funds. You may not even have noticed how high expenses were during the ebullient 1990s when stock and bond funds produced generous double-digit returns. But I believe that we will be very fortunate during the early decades of the 2000s to earn high single-digit returns, and high expenses will dramatically reduce your investment earnings.

In rules 8 and 9, I will recommend broad-based stock and bond index funds as the preferred investment vehicles of choice. Of all the funds offered in the market, index funds have the lowest expense ratios. Moreover, index fund managers are fundamentally "buy and hold" investors. Thus, they avoid the transaction costs that are associated with funds that trade from security to security and regularly turn over the holdings in their portfolios. But even with index funds, expense ratios vary among mutual fund companies. You can be an educated consumer by learning about expense ratios from the Morningstar Mutual Fund Service (at www.morningstar.com) and from the Securities and Exchange Commission (at http://www.sec.gov/investor/tools/mfcc/mfcc-int.htm). Don't let high fund expenses eat up your retirement lunches.

Costs Matter for All Financial Products

Costs are important for all financial products and services. In discussing insurance in Rule 3, I cautioned against buying variable annuities because they were in essence expensive mutual fund products in a costly insurance wrapper. I also advised you to eschew whole life insurance policies in favor of low-fee term insurance policies. Every dollar you pay in fees and commissions for such products is a dollar inevitably lost to you.

If you do buy any stocks directly, you should shop around and have your orders executed by a discount broker. With the advent of competitive commission rates, it has now become possible to buy your brokerage services at wholesale prices. A number of brokers today will execute your stock orders at discounts of as much as 90 percent off the standard commission rates charged by the leading "full-service" brokerage houses. The discount broker usually provides a plain-piperack service. If you want your hand held, if you want opinions on individual stocks and general portfolio advice and investment suggestions, the discount broker may not be for you. If, however, you know exactly what you want to buy, the discount broker can get it for you at much lower commission rates than the standard full-service house. Make sure, however, to ask if your discount broker is transacting your orders for stocks like IBM or Exxon on the New York Stock Exchange. Some discounters actually do the transactions off the exchange, and the net price you end up paying is higher than that charged by a full-service broker. Purely for the execution of stock-market orders, you should use an honest discounter. The discounters all belong to the Security Investors Protection Corporation, which insures all accounts up to $100,000.

You can also make security trades electronically. Electronic trading enables you to buy and sell hundreds of shares of stocks for as little as $7.95 per trade. But let me warn you, few investors who try to trade in and out of stocks each day make profits. Don't let low commission rates seduce you into becoming one of the legion of unsuccessful former day traders.

Don't Get Wrapped Up

While on the subject of commission costs, you should be aware of a Wall Street innovation called the "wrap account." For a single fee, your broker obtains the services of a professional money manager, who then selects for you a portfolio of stocks, bonds, and perhaps real estate. Brokerage commissions and advisory fees are "wrapped" into the overall fee. The costs involved in wrap accounts are extremely high. Annual fees can be as high as 3 percent per year for small accounts, and there may be additional execution fees and fund expenses (if the manager uses mutual funds or REITs). With those kinds of expenses, it will be virtually impossible for you to beat the market. My advice here is: Avoid taking the wrap.

RULE EIGHT

Bow to the Wisdom of the Market

WHO WANTS to admit that an amorphous, inorganic entity such as the financial market is smarter than they are? Certainly not the financial professionals who earn lucrative fees and commissions for telling naive customers that they know best. And certainly not do-it-yourself day traders who know, just absolutely know, that they can pick and choose where few, if any, have profited before.

And yet, the cold, unflattering—and, yes, unexciting—truth is that the financial market, that sprawling clumsy behemoth, is smarter than any individual. Smarter, that is, in that no one can consistently outfox it by predicting its movements. The road to your financial success is paved with this understanding. When you were growing up, you probably heard the phrase, "Mother knows best." Now that you are an investor, remember the phrase, "The market knows best." Neither you nor any guru can consistently beat it over time.

After a career of fifty years in the investment business, Jack Bogle, the founder of the Vanguard Group of Investment Companies, has come to the same conclusion. In his characteristically blunt and direct fashion, Bogle puts it this way:

> It's time to face reality: There is no evidence that research—even the research of the Institutional Investor all-stars—adds value. Academic studies only confirm what we all believe: The stock market is highly efficient, and that stock prices incorporate virtually all information. As I've often said, "Never think you know more than the market. Nobody does."

Since every bit of my academic and practical experience supports Bogle's contention, all I can say is "Amen."

Why the Market Is Smarter Than You Are

Financial economists agree that it is impossible for individual investors to beat the market. Rather than call the market smart, economists are more likely to claim that the market is generally remarkably efficient. In so doing, these people came up with what is known as the efficient-market theory. The theory sometimes appears in its initials only: EMT. Say these letters quickly and it sounds like "empty." But that's another story.

The main premise of the theory is that the stock market is an extraordinarily efficient institution for reflecting without delay any information that arises. When news arises, an army of profit-seeking Wall Street professionals pounces on it rapidly, driving stock prices up or down. As a result, stock prices reflect whatever good or bad news there is about each individual company or about the economy as a whole. Something that everyone knows is not worth knowing. Whatever news you read in the newspapers, hear on television, or receive via the Internet has already been incorporated into stock prices before you are ready to make a trade. By the time you hear the news, the market has already digested it. Thus, it is impossible to select stocks that will outperform the market with any degree of consistency. Hence, the blindfolded chimp throwing darts at the stock pages can select individual stocks as well as the experts. In fact, as I noted earlier, the correct advice is not to use darts to select a few stocks but rather to throw a towel over the stock pages and buy and hold a portfolio representing an index of all the stocks in the market.

If stock prices reflect information without delay, then prices will change with the receipt of new information. But true "news" must itself be unpredictable and random. Otherwise, it wouldn't be news at all. Tomorrow's price movements must then be unpredictable since any information that might have been used to predict tomorrow's price has already been reflected today. If I know a company will be worth more tomorrow, I will bid up the price today. Paradoxically, then, the more efficient a stock market is, the more unpredictable it will be. It's not that prices move capriciously—it's rather because really new information arises in an unpredictable fashion. And so market prices (except for the long-term up trend reflecting the growth in the economy) move like a drunkard meandering down the street. This is what financial economists mean when they say that stock-market prices in an efficient market behave like a random walk.

On Wall Street, the terms "random walk" and "efficient market" are obscenities. You can easily understand why. The logical conclusion of a belief that markets are efficient is to fire your professional manager and buy a low-cost index fund that simply mimics the performance of a broad stock-market index. Obviously, Wall Street pros don't like being compared to bare-assed apes throwing darts. They certainly will not accept a theory that claims that all their investment advice, earnings projections, and esoteric charts are worthless. In fact, professional "advice" is often worth less than zero since it induces investors to pay fees that are too high, undertake investment strategies that involve costly transactions charges, and pay more in taxes than they need to.

One of the most savvy market commentators, Jason Zweig, sums up the situation as follows:

> As I traipse around the country speaking to investing groups, or just stay in my cage writing my articles, I'm often accused of "disempowering" people because I refuse to give any credence to anyone's hope of beating the market. The knowledge that I don't need to know anything is an incredibly profound form of knowledge. Personally, I think it's the ultimate form of empowerment. If you can plug your ears to every attempt (by anyone) to predict what the markets will do, you will outperform nearly every other investor alive over the long run. Only the mantra of "don't know, and I don't care" will get you there.

Being Smarter Doesn't Always Mean Being Smart

Are there any exceptions to the theory? Are there times when the market is flat-out stupid and gets it wrong? Yes, the market does make mistakes from time to time. The Internet bubble that popped in early 2000 is a classic example. In my view, it was a time of mass insanity—like financial mad cow disease. But don't for a minute think that professional advice would have gotten you out of the stock market at the top and into cash. Quite the contrary. At the top of the market, professionally managed mutual funds had the lowest cash positions in over thirty years. And the leading fund managers loaded up their funds with precisely those Internet and high-tech stocks that proved to be the most overpriced stocks in the market. After the fact, we know that the market does make mistakes, just as we know Monday morning what play the quarterback should have called. But don't count on professional advisors to help you time the market. They promise something they cannot deliver.

Timing Isn't Everything

No one can time the market. As the legendary investor Bernard Baruch once put it: "Only liars manage always to be out during bad times and in during good times." The only way you can be sure to be there when lightning strikes is to stay fully invested.

Or, as financial observer Charles Ellis puts it, "Investors would do well to learn from deer hunters and fishermen who know the importance of being there and using patient persistence—so they are there when opportunity knocks."

Ellis shows in the chart below that over an eighteen-year period from 1982 to 2000, an investor who stayed fully invested in the S&P 500-Stock Index made an average annual return of more than 18 percent. But if he or she had missed the best thirty days in the market, the return would have been only 11.2 percent.

COMPOUND RETURNS (%), 1982–2000

Courtesy of Cambridge Associates.

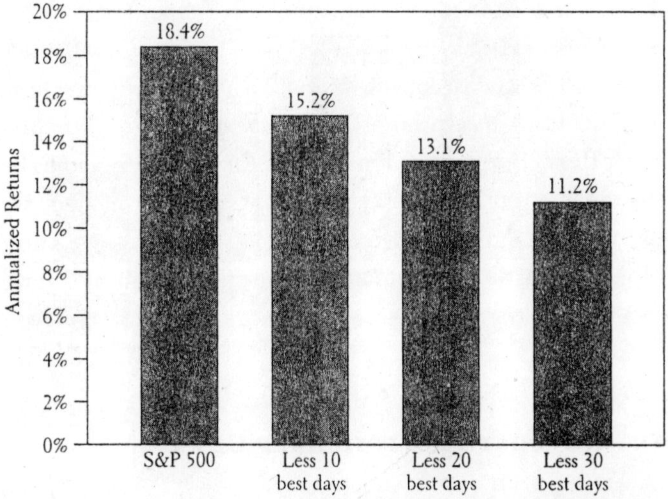

Source: Charles Ellis, *Winning the Loser's Game.*

Ellis also studied the period from 1928 to 2000, when one dollar invested in stocks grew to $1,600. He showed that removing just the five best days out of seventy-two years reduced an investor's return substantially. As the illustration in the chart below shows, if you were out of the market during the three years 1933, 1954, and 1985 (years when pessimism among the pros was ubiquitous), your final stake would have been almost 75 percent lower. Ellis concludes: "Market timing is a wicked idea: Don't try it—ever."

Cumulative Returns on One Dollar Invested, 1928–2000

Courtesy of Cambridge Associates, Datastream International, and McGraw-Hill.

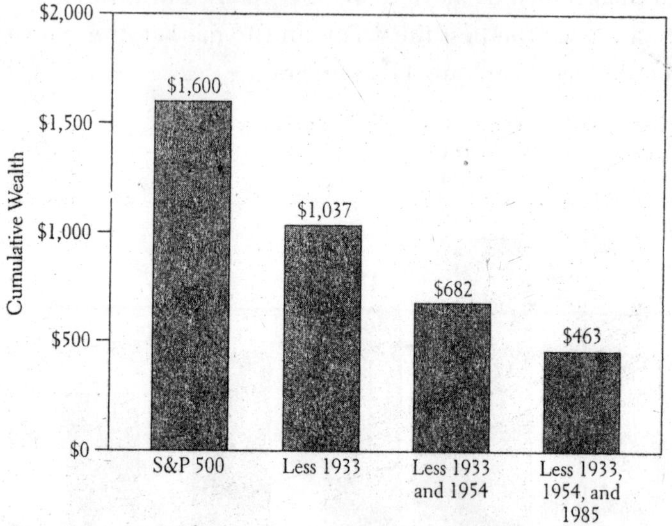

Source: Charles Ellis, *Winning the Loser's Game.*

Why Do Most Professionals Get C's?

I have believed in the efficient-market theory for over thirty years. As more and more evidence accumulates, I am more convinced than ever. The broad stock-market indexes have regularly outperformed two thirds or more of the actively managed funds. The indexes wracked up an even better case over the past twenty years, when they beat the performance of over 80 percent of professional actively managed mutual funds. Garry Trudeau had it right in the *Doonesbury* cartoon:

Not only do most mutual funds underperform the broad stock-market index, but the amount by which they do so is staggeringly large. The table below shows that well over three quarters of the typical actively managed equity funds underperform the S&P 500 stock market. It is one of the great myths of the investment business that professional managers can beat the market. Rex Sinquefield of Dimensional Fund Advisors puts it in a particularly brutal way: "There are three classes of people who do not believe that markets work: the Cubans, the North Koreans, and active managers."

The Index Wins

	*10 Yrs**	*20 Yrs**
Percent of large capitalization equity funds outperformed by the S&P 500 Index	84%	88%

* Ending December 31, 2002

More dramatic evidence of the superiority of a strategy of simply buying the index is shown in the next table. Here we look at the returns of the average actively managed equity mutual fund compared with the returns from the S&P 500 Index. The index wins by over 2 percentage points per year.

Comparison of Returns: Average Equity Fund vs. S&P 500 Index

Periods Ending December 31, 2002

	10 Yrs	*20 Yrs*
S&P 500 Index	9.27%	12.46%
Average equity fund*	7.18%	10.04%
S&P 500 Advantage	2.09%	2.42%

* Consists of all Lipper equity categories

Source: Lipper, Wilshire, and The Vanguard Group.

How can this be? In terms of stock-market trading, professional investors make up something like 90 percent of the volume in the stock exchanges. In a real sense today, professional investors are the market. And since all of the outstanding shares have to be held by someone, it stands to reason that it is professionals who now own almost all the shares. (Sure, individuals may be the ultimate owners through their 401[k] and other pension plans, but they own the shares only indirectly.) Well, if professional investors such as mutual fund managers and pension fund managers own essentially all of the shares, they should earn the market return. Clearly, if you add up all the players in the stock market, they must by definition earn the market return. They can't be like Garrison Keillor's Lake Wobegon, where all the children are good-looking and everyone is above average.

The fact is that they do earn the market return before expenses. It is their expenses that drag their return down below that available from the market as a whole. In the mutual fund arena, actively managed funds tend to have expense ratios of close to 1.5 percentage points (or 150 basis points). Index mutual funds can be managed for only a tenth of that amount.

In addition, active portfolio managers tend to turn over their portfolios about once a year, incurring large transactions costs. They must pay not only brokerage commissions (the smallest part of the cost of the transactions) but also the spreads between the bid and asked prices of the middlemen who make up the market, as well as "market impact costs." The latter costs reflect the fact that when a big institutional investor begins to buy or sell a stock, its price tends to rise or fall before the institution can complete its transaction. All told, transactions costs tend to add another half of 1 percent (50 basis points) to the costs of running a professionally managed fund. In total, expenses siphon off somewhat more than 2 percentage points from the net return investors receive. Actively managed funds underperform the market by essentially the amount of their management fees and transactions expenses. The individual who buys an actively managed fund pays dearly for poor performance. The monies paid for such expenses go directly to the croupiers—not to your retirement fund. Actively managed funds don't beat the market. The market beats them.

But Don't Some Active Managers Beat the Market Every Year?

In any period, be it the last quarter, the last year, or the last decade, there are some professional managers who do beat the market. These are the managers who get written up in the financial press with the accolades usually accorded to rock stars. Why not just pick the managers who have demonstrated superior performance? Why not bet on the best jockeys? Isn't this the sure route to superior performance?

The problem is that there is no persistency to good performance—it is as random as the market. If a manager beats an index in one period, there's absolutely no guarantee that the performance will be repeated in the next. I have examined the lack of persistency in fund returns over periods from the 1960s through the early 2000s. The top funds of the sixties had dismal performances in the seventies, and most of them went out of business. The top funds of the seventies (those that actually did beat the market) badly underperformed the market in the eighties. And the top funds of the eighties underperformed in the nineties.

Let's look at a recent example to show how ephemeral and fleeting investment prowess really is. In the table below, I show the top twenty mutual funds for the three-year period 1997 through 1999. These were the funds that were written up in the financial press as "the funds to buy for the new millennium." They produced returns twice as large as the market as a whole. Who would want to buy a boring index fund when they could have access to real investment genius? And indeed new mutual fund investments by individuals flowed largely into these "hot" funds. The table then examines the records of these funds during the next three-year period, 2000–02. Yesterday's genius turned into today's disaster. Those top funds' performance declined twice as much as the market as a whole, producing punishing losses for investors.

Getting Burned by Hot Funds

Fund Name	1997–1999 *Rank*	1997–1999 *Average Annual Return (%)*	2000–2002 *Rank**	2000–2002 *Average Annual Return (%)*
Rydex: OTC Fund; Investor Shares	1	65.82	841	–37.07
RS Inv: Emerg Growth	2	62.46	832	–31.17
Morgan Stanley Capital Opportunity: B	3	59.47	845	–40.72
Janus Olympus Fund	4	58.49	791	–27.42
Janus Twenty	5	54.79	801	–28.63
Managers: Capital Appreciation	6	53.28	798	–28.20
Janus Mercury	7	51.51	790	–27.24
Fidelity Aggressive Growth	8	51.46	843	–39.09
Van Wagoner: Emerging Growth: A	9	50.05	851	–51.66
WM: Growth: A	10	49.67	793	–27.88
Janus Venture	11	49.56	819	–29.70
Van Kampen Emerging Growth: A	12	49.34	785	–26.38
Fidelity New Millennium	13	49.22	500	–14.90
PBHG: Select Equity	14	49.14	837	–33.45
PBHG: Janus Enterprise	15	48.71	836	–33.11
TCW Galileo: SC Growth	16	45.95	844	–39.32
Morgan Stanley Inst: Mid-Cap Growth	17	45.42	735	–23.28
Morgan Stanley Special Growth: B	18	45.34	846	–41.46
IDEX: Jan Growth: T	19	44.96	802	–28.70
ING: Small Cap Opportunity: B	20	44.06	826	–30.64
Average Top 20		51.44		–32.00
S&P 500 Return		**27.56**		**–14.55**

*Out of 851 funds with at least $100 million in assets

Source: Bogle Financial Research Center.

It is true there are always some funds that do beat the market, just as there are always some stocks that produce above-average returns. But I have always said that if picking stocks is a random walk down Wall Street, picking funds is an obstacle course through Hell's Kitchen. There is no way to choose the best managers in advance. I have calculated the results of employing strategies of buying the funds with the best recent-year performance, best recent two-year performance, best five-year and ten-year performance, and not one of these strategies produced above-average returns. I calculated the returns from buying the best funds selected by *Forbes* magazine—the Forbes Honor Roll funds—and found that these funds subsequently produced below-average returns. The chart below tabulates the returns from the Morningstar Rating Service's best funds (their so-called 5-Star funds). As the chart demon-

UNDERACHIEVERS

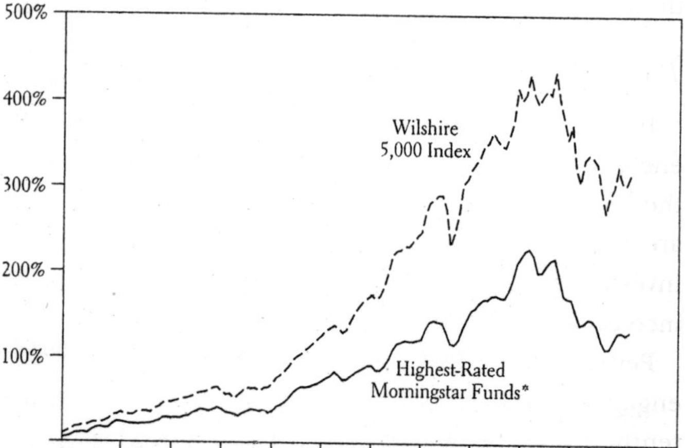

*Based on equal investment in 55 funds, after expenses, loads, and redemption fees

Source: *Hulbert Financial Digest*

strates, you would be much better off in an index fund than buying a portfolio of Morningstar's 5-Star funds. Chasing hot performance is a costly and self-defeating exercise. As Jonathan Clements of the *Wall Street Journal* quips: "When an investor says 'I own last year's best performing fund' he usually forgets to add 'unfortunately, I bought it this year.'"

Managers Who Deserve an A

Of course there are exceptions. Whenever I talk about the failure of professional managers to beat the market, there is always someone in the back of the room who pipes up: "What about Warren Buffett and Peter Lynch?" It is true that both Buffett and Lynch compiled extraordinary investment records, and if you had invested your money with them, you would have beaten the market. Are they living proof that my thesis is incorrect? I don't think so, for three reasons.

1. The Role of Chance

In any activity in which large numbers of people are engaged, although the average is likely to predominate, the unexpected is bound to happen. The fact that there are a very small number of really good performers in the investment management business actually is not at all inconsistent with the laws of chance.

Perhaps the laws of chance should be illustrated. Let's engage in a coin-flipping contest. Those who can consistently flip heads will be declared winners. The contest begins and 1,000 contestants flip coins. Just as would be expected by chance, 500 of them flip heads, and these winners are allowed to advance to the second stage of the contest and flip again. As might be expected, 250 flip heads. Operating under the laws of chance, there will be 125 winners in the third round, 63 in the fourth, 31 in the fifth, 16 in the sixth, and 8 in the seventh.

By this time, crowds start to gather to witness the surprising ability of these expert coin-flippers. The winners are overwhelmed with adulation. They are celebrated as geniuses in the art of coin-flipping, their biographies are written, and people urgently seek their advice. After all, there were 1,000 contestants and only 8 could consistently flip heads. The game continues, and some contestants eventually flip heads nine and ten times in a row. If we had let the losers continue to play (as mutual fund managers do, even after a bad year), we would have found several more contestants who flipped eight or nine heads out of ten and were therefore regarded as expert coin-flippers. The point of this analogy is not to indicate that investment fund managers can or should make their decisions by flipping coins, but that the laws of chance do operate, and they can explain some amazing success stories.

As long as there are averages, some people will beat them. With large numbers of players in the money game, and there are more than 5,000 individual mutual funds, chance will—and does—explain some super performance records. The very great publicity given occasional success in stock selection reminds me of the story of the doctor who claimed he had developed a cure for cancer in chickens. He proudly announced that in 33 percent of the cases tested, remarkable improvement was noted. In another one third of the cases, he admitted, there seemed to be no change in condition. He then rather sheepishly added, "And I'm afraid the third chicken ran away."

2. They Did It Their Way

Of all the professional asset managers, Warren Buffett's record is clearly the most extraordinary. From 1965 to the present, Buffett's company, Berkshire Hathaway, has earned investment returns about double those for the market as whole. But that record was not achieved by superior stock picking, as it is often portrayed in the press. Warren Buffett is a consummate businessman more than a stock-picker. He has often taken a very active role in the businesses in which he has invested. One of his earliest investments was in the Washington Post Company. According to Katharine Graham, the paper's chief executive, Buffett played the critical role in saving the paper from financial disaster and in turning the stock into a profitable investment. So it was in many of Berkshire Hathaway's most successful investments. And when an error was made in the case of Buffett's investment in the investment firm Salomon Brothers, Buffett himself became the firm's leader to save it from liquidation. Warren Buffett is an extraordinary business leader, and he would be one of the first people to advise that most people would be far better off simply investing in index funds.

The record of Peter Lynch, the photogenic spokesperson for the Fidelity Group, is less impressive. Most of the outsized returns from his Magellan Fund occurred when the fund was very small (indeed some of them occurred even before the fund was open to the public). What a number of mutual fund complexes do is to start, say, ten small new funds, called incubator funds. Suppose two or three of them do better than the market; the mutual fund complex then kills off the seven or eight that did poorly (these are merged into successful funds, thus killing off the poor records) and heavily advertises the two or three that did well. As the Magellan Fund grew, its superiority to the market diminished sharply. It is very hard for a multibillion-dollar fund to distinguish itself. What Peter Lynch did then was absolute genius: He quit when he was ahead. In 1990, at the ripe old age of forty-six, he retired from running Magellan. By retiring at the peak of his performance, he guaranteed himself membership in the portfolio managers' Hall of Fame.

3. You Never Know in Advance Who the Winners Will Be

I am convinced that over the next twenty to thirty years there will be other very successful managers like Warren Buffett and Peter Lynch. But neither you nor I can possibly know in advance who they will be. The fact that good past performance of a mutual fund is generally no help in predicting future performance only serves to emphasize this point. The table on page 129 shows just how inconsistent fund performance can be. Thus, my advice is that rather than futilely attempting to find that needle in the haystack, buy the haystack (in the form of a broad-based index fund) instead.

RULE NINE

Back Proven Winners: Model Portfolios of Index Funds

BY NOW you know that there is no magic formula to obtain enormous riches with no initial stake. You know that it takes more than the "The Courage to Be Rich," as one popular book suggests. It takes self-sacrifice, stick-to-itiveness, and time. You know that while one in a million may get wealthy by hitting the lottery or the pick-six at the racetrack, most people accomplish nothing but losing the modest amounts each week that they spend on tickets and that could with the proper strategy amount to a significant portfolio over time.

You also know that our securities markets are enormously efficient and that the investment experts you read about and watch being interviewed on TV cannot produce above-average returns. In fact, they charge high expenses and actually underperform a totally unmanaged index fund, one that charges low expenses and simply buys and holds all the stocks available in the market. There are no investment gurus. The secret of successful investing is that there is no secret. By just hitching your savings to the market as a whole, you will over time do better than 90 percent of all investors, including the pros. No other investment strategy can make such a guarantee. Owning index funds of the various asset classes is the ultimate risk reducer and diversifier. In this rule, I'll show you how to follow a simple scheme to put your savings and investments on the right path to achieve financial security.

The Index Advantage

Let's first summarize the arguments for investing your retirement money in index funds. Index investing is nothing more than a strategy of buying a fund that holds all, or a representative sample of all, the stocks in a broad stock-market index. This simple strategy has outperformed all but a tiny handful of the thousands of equity mutual funds that are sold to the public.

Let's list all the advantages of an index fund strategy:

- Index funds simplify investing. You don't have to choose among the thousands of individual stocks and mutual funds available to the public.
- Index funds are cost-efficient. Those that I recommend below have no sales charges and have minuscule expense charges. Moreover, index funds do a minimal amount of trading. Thus, they avoid the very heavy transactions costs of actively managed funds, which tend to turn over their entire portfolio about once a year.

- Index funds regularly produce higher returns for investors than do actively managed funds.
- Index funds are predictable. You know beyond doubt that you will earn the rate of return provided by the stock market. Yes, you will lose money when the market declines, but you will never own the fund that performs several times worse then the market.
- Index funds are tax-efficient. If you do own stocks in taxable accounts (that is, outside your IRA or retirement plan), then you need to invest in index funds that don't trade from security to security and therefore don't tend to generate taxable gains.

It's true that when you buy an index fund, you give up the chance to boast at the golf course that you picked the best performing stock or mutual fund. That's why some critics claim that indexing relegates your results to mediocrity. In fact, you are virtually guaranteed to do better than average. It's like going out on the golf course and shooting every round at par. How many golfers can do better than that? Index funds provide a simple low-cost solution to your investing problem.

Sure, the laws of chance alone will result in your reading about some funds that outperform the broad stock-market indexes in each quarter and each year. But there is no persistence to above-average performance. The past track record of a mutual fund cannot tell you how well the fund will do in the future, with one exception. What we do know is that equity funds that have particularly high annual expense charges (up to 2 percentage points per year) are likely to do especially poorly because their very high expenses will persistently drag down performance. But the top ratings of *Morningstar*, *Value Line*, *Forbes*, and the various investment magazines cannot tell you how funds will perform in the future. Just because your fund was especially good yesterday, there is no reason to think it will continue to be good tomorrow. And even if some young Warren Buffetts and Peter Lynches are out there today, there is no way you will be able to identify them before the fact.

But Not All Index Funds Are Alike

Some investment advisers may recommend index funds but try to argue that you need professional advice to tell you what index funds you should buy. After all, there are hundreds of different types of index funds covering not only stocks but bonds and real estate as well. Some equity funds concentrate on big companies (so-called large-capitalization stocks) while others concentrate on small companies (small-cap stocks). There are even indexes representing middle-sized (mid-cap) stocks. Also, some index funds track so-called value indexes. This means that the index includes stocks that tend to sell at low prices relative to their earnings or to the value of their assets. Others track "growth" indexes, including stocks selling at high prices relative to earnings and assets but that promise high future growth. Then there are small-cap value index funds and large-cap growth funds. Among bond index funds, you have a wide menu of choices ranging from very safe short-term government bonds to risky high-yield corporate bonds. I have seen books with the most complicated recommendations advising individuals to mix eight to ten of these funds so as to obtain adequate diversification.

There is no need at all to complicate your investments in this way. What you need is a single stock fund that buys and holds virtually *all* the stocks in the market and a bond index fund that buys a portfolio comprising *all* the bonds in the market. By purchasing the broadest-based equity index fund, an investor will automatically be invested in both large and small companies as well as in "value" and "growth" stocks and will be represented in all the different industry groups. These broad-based index funds are typically called "Total Stock Market" funds. The indexes they track are either the Wilshire 5,000-Total Stock Market Index or the Russell 3,000 Index, which comprise essentially all the stocks available in the market. Below, I will list a sample of such funds that would make suitable investments.

Exchange Traded Funds

One of the newest and fastest growing sets of financial products available is called exchange traded funds (ETFs). I'm a fan of these funds because they are exactly the kind of index funds that I think are the very best vehicles for savings and retirement funds. But for most investors I don't recommend them. Let me explain what they are and why most people would be better off with regular index mutual funds rather than ETFs.

Exchange traded funds are index funds that trade on the major stock exchanges just like individual stocks. The most popular is the NASDAQ 100, known by its ticker symbol QQQ, or by its nickname, the "cubes." This fund is an index of the NASDAQ 100 stocks, the hundred largest and best-known securities traded on the NASDAQ exchange. It includes companies such as Microsoft, Cisco, Intel, and eBay—mainly the New Economy high-tech companies that many investors expect will be the biggest growers over the next decades. The other very popular ETF is called the "Spyder," the peculiar spelling taken from its ticker symbol SPY. This ETF tracks the Standard & Poor's 500-Stock Market Index. There are even competing S&P 500 ETFs, one issued by State Street Investors and the other by Barclay Global Investors. ETFs also exist for the Dow Jones Industrial Average (called Diamonds); for various industry groups (or sectors) called Sector Spyders; and for various foreign countries. There is even a "Total Stock Market" index ETF, called a Viper.

ETFs do have advantages over indexed mutual funds. They enable an investor to buy and sell at any time during the day and thus have advantages for traders. They also have very low expense ratios and many have some slight advantage for taxable investors in terms of their tax efficiency because of their ability to redeem shares without generating a taxable event.

The problem with ETFs arises when an individual is making periodic payments into a retirement savings plan, as is the normal case for people with IRAs and other tax-advantaged plans. Every payment into the plan will incur a transaction charge if ETFs are used. The individual will have to pay a brokerage charge (which can be a substantial percentage of the amount invested even if a discount broker is used) as well as a dealer's spread between the price at which you can buy an ETF and the price at which you can sell it. With a no-load mutual fund, no transactions charges are involved. Moreover, with a mutual fund, any dividends paid by the index fund will be automatically invested. With an ETF, additional transactions charges can be involved when you reinvest your dividends. Thus, most individuals who are saving and investing modest monthly or quarterly amounts will find the index mutual fund to be the preferred investment vehicle.

Indexing Works for Bonds, Real Estate, and Other Asset Classes

I have suggested that investors will want to reduce risk by buying a portfolio of stocks, not just a few stocks. Of course, index funds fit the bill since they entail broad diversification over the whole market. I also indicated that a diversified low-risk investment plan will include other asset classes such as bonds and real estate in addition to stocks. When stocks go down as they did in the early 2000s, a portfolio with bonds and real estate is far more stable. Bonds and real estate equities rose during that period, offsetting the general decline in stock prices. What you want in the various other asset classes is some investments that tend to zig while your portfolio of stocks may zag.

Fortunately, index funds exist that mimic the performance of the bond market and the real estate market. They, too, are low-cost with no sales charges. And they, too, beat actively managed bond and real estate mutual funds hands down. The majority of actively managed bond funds are outperformed by an index fund holding a broad selection of corporate and government bonds. Similarly, an index fund that holds a portfolio of essentially all the existing real estate investment trusts (REITs) has generally outperformed actively managed funds of REITs.

Index funds also tend to outperform actively managed funds that hold international securities. This is even true for active managers in emerging market stocks, where many professionals suggest that markets are less efficient. Paradoxically, the less efficient trading markets in emerging economies make indexing particularly useful. In markets where illiquidity is the rule and where dealer spreads between bid and offered prices are wide, a passive strategy is particularly effective because it avoids significant transactions costs that can drag down returns.

I do recommend that investors with substantial resources supplement a broad-based U.S. stock index with one that invests in stocks from the world economies outside the United States. One broad-based non-U.S. developed country index fund tracks the EAFE index (the index of stocks from Europe, Australasia, and the Far East). An index that includes stocks in the developing economies is the Morgan Stanley Capital International Emerging Markets Index, and there are funds that track that index. But for most people of modest means, as I suggested in Rule 6, you can get along fine by just investing in U.S. companies.

What Index and What Funds Should Be Chosen?

Let's first consider common stocks. Should you try to match one of the most popular indexes such as the Dow Jones Average of 30 stocks or the Standard & Poor's Index of 500 stocks? In fact, most investment money that is indexed does try to replicate the S&P 500 Index. My recommendation is that you use a much broader index such as the Russell 3,000 or the Wilshire 5,000. Funds that use these broader indexes are usually called "Total Stock Market" index funds.

There are two reasons for my recommendation. First, the S&P indexing strategy has become so popular that it may have affected the pricing of the component stocks in the index. This can clearly be seen when changes are made in the composition of the index, as unavoidably happens from time to time. When some companies are merged out of existence (such as Compaq computer, which merged with Hewlett Packard) or failed (such as Enron), new companies must be added to the index. It turns out that newly included companies tended to appreciate in price (at least temporarily) by more than 5 percent—simply because they are now a part of the S&P Index. Portfolio managers who run index funds are required to incur transactions costs to purchase the stocks of the new companies (in proportion to their relative size and, therefore, their weight in the index) so that their portfolio's performance will continue to conform to that of the index. Thus, the very popularity of S&P 500 indexing can make the stocks included in the index a bit pricier than comparable non-S&P Index stocks, at least for some period of time, and can hurt the performance of investors since these stocks must be purchased at temporarily inflated prices. And in recent years, there have been an increasing number of index changes requiring considerable transactions for what should be a passively run fund.

There is a second reason to favor a broader, more inclusive index. Seventy-five years of market history confirms that, in the aggregate, smaller stocks have tended to outperform larger ones. For example, from 1926 to 2002, a portfolio of smaller stocks produced a rate of return of more than 1 percentage point more than the return from larger stocks (such as those in the S&P 500). Although the smaller stocks were undoubtedly riskier than the major blue chips, the point is that a well-diversified portfolio of small companies is likely to produce somewhat enhanced returns.

The S&P 500 represents about 75 to 80 percent of the market value of all outstanding U.S. common stocks. Literally thousands of companies represent the remaining 20 to 25 percent of the total U.S. market value. These are in many cases the emerging growth companies that offer higher investment rewards (as well as higher risks). The Wilshire 5,000 Index contains all publicly traded U.S. common stocks on the New York and American stock exchanges and in the NASDAQ market—in all, more than 6,000 securities. As such, it is the best representation available of the entire U.S. market. And when you buy a "Total Stock Market" index fund, you avoid being in one of the S&P 500 Funds that must make transactions to buy the small growth companies that get large enough to be included in the S&P 500. You will already own those companies because you own all the companies in the market.

The table below lists a number of "Total Stock Market" index funds that have no sales charges and a low annual expense ratio. You should limit your selection to such no-load, low-expense funds. All index funds are not created equal. Some have unconscionably high expenses. The main advantage of a passively managed fund is its minimal expenses. If you are investing through a retirement plan at work and no index funds are offered in your plan, petition your human resources department to add such an option to your investment choices. Most companies do offer such an option.

Data on Selected Total Stock Market Index Funds 2003

Fund Name	*Index*	*Maximum Sales Charge (%)*	*Minimum Initial Purchase ($) (IRA minimum)*	*Minimum Subsequent Purchase ($)*	*Recent Expense Ratio*	*Payroll Deduction*	*Keogh Plan Available*	*IRA Plan Available*
Fidelity Spartan Total Index www.fidelity.com 800-343-3548	Wilshire 5,000	None	$15,000 ($15,000)	$1,000	0.25	Yes	Yes	Yes
Schwab 1000 Investor www.schwab.com 800-435-4000	Custom Index	None	$2,500 ($1,000)	$500	0.46	Yes	Yes	Yes
T Rowe Price Total Equity Market Index www.troweprice.com 800-638-5660	Wilshire 5,000	None	$2,500 ($1,000)	$100	0.40	Yes	Yes	Yes
TIAA-CREF Equity Index Fund www.TIAA-CREF.org 800-842-1924	Russell 3,000	None	$2,500 ($2,000)	$50	0.26	Yes*	No	Yes
Vanguard Total Stock Market Index† www.vanguard.com 800-662-7447	Wilshire 5,000	None	$3,000 ($1,000)	$100	0.20	Yes	Yes	Yes

* Select employers   † I serve on the board of directors of this fund.

In Rule 6, I suggested that most people of modest means are likely to do reasonably well by purchasing one domestic "Total Stock Market" index fund as their sole vehicle for investing in common stocks. Certainly, such a plan will simplify the investment process. Those with substantial assets, however, may want to diversify their stock holdings even further and add a "Total International Stock Index Fund" for up to one quarter of their equity exposure. Such funds can be obtained from some of the mutual fund complexes listed in the preceding table; you can request a prospectus and an application through their Web site and 800 numbers shown in the table.

Just as I recommend stock index funds, I also recommend bond index funds. Again, avoid any fund with a sales charge (or load fee) and look for a fund with a low expense ratio. The table below presents a sample of excellent choices. Again, if your 401(k) plan does not offer a bond index fund, ask your employer to include one.

I recommend an indexing approach for real estate equities as well. Unfortunately, there is only one REIT index fund available to the public. Therefore, in the table below I have included three of the major actively managed REIT funds that have reasonably low expenses and a competitive long-term record.

A Life-Cycle Guide to Asset Allocation

In the pages that follow, I present a life-cycle guide to asset allocation. These recommendations have appeared in recent editions of my longer book, *A Random Walk Down Wall Street.*

Data on Selected Bond Index Funds 2003

Fund Name	Maximum Sales Charge (%)	Minimum Initial Purchase ($) (IRA minimum)	Minimum Subsequent Purchase ($) (IRA minimum)	Recent Expense Ratio	Payroll Deduction	Keogh Plan Available	IRA Plan Available
Dreyfus Bond Market Index-Basic www.dreyfus.com 800-373-9387	None	$10,000 ($5,000)	$1,000	0.40	Yes	Yes	Yes
Schwab Total Bond Market Index www.schwab.com 800-435-4000	None	$1,000 ($500)	$100	0.20	Yes	Yes	Yes
USAA Income Fund www.usaa.com 800-531-8181	None	$3,000 ($250)	$50	0.41	Yes	Yes	Yes
Vanguard Total Bond Market Index Fund* www.vanguard.com 800-662-7447	None	$3,000 ($1,000)	$100	0.22	Yes	Yes	Yes

* I serve on the board of directors of this fund.

Data on Selected Real Estate Mutual Funds 2003

Fund Name	*Maximum Sales Charge (%)*	*Minimum Initial Purchase ($) (IRA minimum)*	*Minimum Subsequent Purchase ($)*	*Recent Expense Ratio*	*Payroll Deduction*	*Keogh Plan Available*	*IRA Plan Available*
Cohen & Steers Realty www.cohenandsteers.com 800-437-9912	No	$10,000 (NA)	$500	1.08	No	No	No
Fidelity Real Estate www.fidelity.com 800-544-6666	No*	$2,500 ($2,500)	$250	0.84	Yes	Yes	Yes
TIAA-CREF Real Estate Securities Fund www.TIAA-CREF.org 800-842-1924	No	$2,500 ($2,000)	$50	0.45	Yes†	No	Yes
Vanguard REIT Index Fund** www.vanguard.com 800-662-7447	No	$3,000 ($1,000)	$100	0.28	Yes	Yes	Yes

*0.75% redemption fee on shares sold within 90 days of purchase †Select employers

**I serve on the board of directors of this fund.

In the Talmud, Rabbi Isaac said that one should always divide his wealth into three parts: a third in land; a third in merchandise (business); and a third ready-at-hand (in liquid form). Such an asset allocation is hardly unreasonable, but we can improve on this ancient advice because we have more refined instruments and a greater appreciation of the considerations that make different asset allocations appropriate for different people. The general ideas behind the recommendations have been spelled out in Rule 5.

For investors in their twenties, a very aggressive investment portfolio is recommended. At this age, you have lots of time to ride out the peaks and valleys of investment cycles, and you have a lifetime of earnings from employment ahead of you.

As investors age, they should start cutting back on riskier investments and start increasing the proportion of the portfolio committed to bonds and stocks that pay generous dividends such as REITs. By the age of fifty-five, investors should start thinking about the transition to retirement and moving the portfolio toward income production. The proportion of bonds increases and the stock portfolio includes a larger proportion of real estate equities. In retirement, three quarters of the portfolio should be in cash, bonds, and real estate, all of which should produce regular income. Nevertheless, even in one's late sixties, 25 percent of the portfolio should be committed to regular stocks and 15 percent to real estate equities (REITs) to give some income growth to cope with inflation.

Life-Cycle Investment Guide
Recommended Asset or Savings Allocations

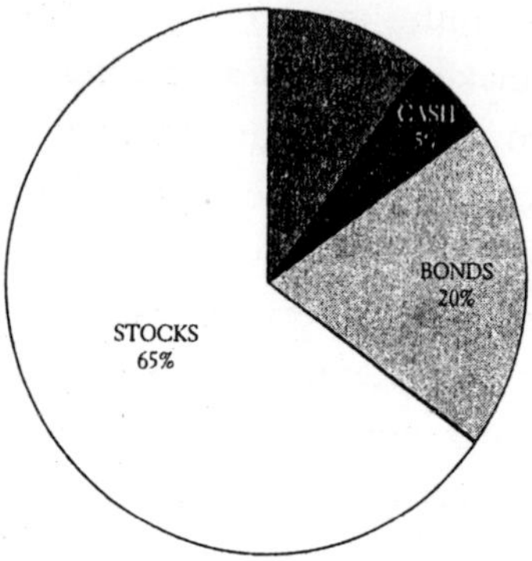

Age: Mid-Twenties

Lifestyle: Fast, aggressive. With a steady stream of earnings, capacity for risk is fairly high. Need discipline of payroll savings to build nest egg.

CASH (5%): money-market fund or short-term-bond fund (average maturity 1 to 1½ years).

BONDS (20%): zero-coupon Treasury bonds, no-load GNMA funds, or no-load high-grade bond fund, some Treasury inflation protection securities (5% of portfolio).*

STOCKS (65%): two-thirds in U.S. stocks with good representation of smaller growth companies; one-third international stocks, including emerging markets.

REAL ESTATE (10%): portfolio of REITs or real estate fund.

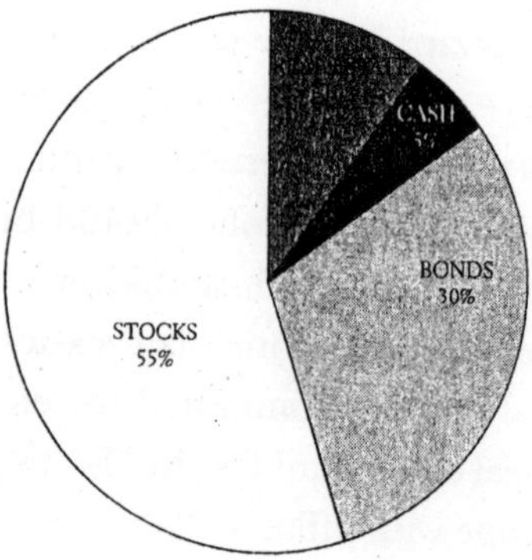

Age: Late Thirties to Early Forties

Lifestyle: Midlife crisis. For childless career couples, capacity for risk is still quite high. Risk options vanishing for those with college tuitions looming.

CASH (5%): money-market fund or short-term-bond fund (average maturity 1 to 1½ years).

BONDS (30%): zero-coupon Treasury bonds, no-load GNMA funds, or no-load high-grade bond fund, some Treasury inflation protection securities (5% of portfolio).*

STOCKS (55%): two-thirds in U.S. stocks with good representation of smaller growth companies; one-third international stocks, including emerging markets.

REAL ESTATE (10%): portfolio of REITs or real estate fund.

*If bonds are to be held outside of tax-favored retirement plans, tax-exempt bonds should be used.

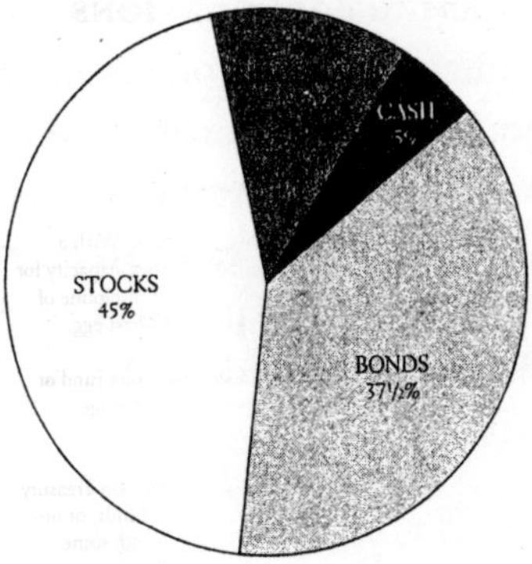

Age: Mid-Fifties

Lifestyle: Many still reeling from college tuitions. No matter what the lifestyle, this age group must start thinking about retirement and the need for income protection.

- CASH (5%): money-market fund or short-term-bond fund (average maturity 1 to 1½ years).
- BONDS (37½%): zero-coupon Treasury bonds, no-load GNMA funds, or no-load high-grade bond fund, some Treasury inflation protection securities (5% of portfolio).*
- STOCKS (45%): three-quarters in U.S. stocks with good representation of smaller growth companies; one-quarter international stocks, including emerging markets.
- REAL ESTATE (12½%): portfolio of REITs or real estate fund.

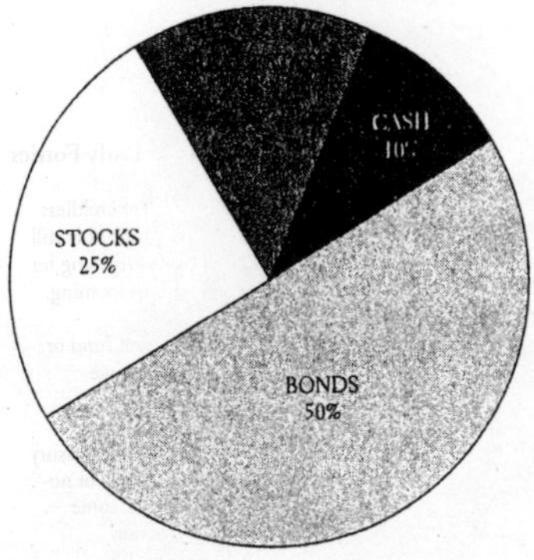

Age: Late Sixties and Beyond

Lifestyle: Enjoying leisure activities but also guarding against major health costs. Little or no capacity for risk.

- CASH (10%): money-market fund or short-term-bond fund (average maturity 1 to 1½ years).
- BONDS (50%): zero-coupon Treasury bonds, no-load GNMA funds, or no-load high-grade bond fund, some Treasury inflation protection securities (5% of portfolio).*
- STOCKS (25%): primarily high-quality U.S. stocks with some representation of smaller growth companies.
- REAL ESTATE (15%): portfolio of REITs or real estate fund.

*If bonds are to be held outside of tax-favored retirement plans, tax-exempt bonds should be used.

Remember also that I am assuming here that you hold most if not all of your securities in tax-advantaged retirement plans. Certainly all of your bonds should be held in such accounts. To the extent that bonds are held outside retirement accounts, you may well prefer to purchase tax-exempt bonds rather than the taxable fixed-income securities. Moreover, you will want to adjust my allocations according to your temperament. Even if you are young, have steady employment and thus a high capacity for risk, a heavy stock allocation might not be for you if your temperament is very risk intolerant. If you can't stand the invariable ups and particularly the sharp downs of the stock market, do as J. P. Morgan suggested—sell down to the sleeping point.

RULE TEN

Don't Be Your Own Worst Enemy: Avoid Stupid Investor Tricks

NIGHT OWLS like myself often watch the late night TV shows. One of the funnier bits from David Letterman's show is the segment called "Stupid Pet Tricks," where pet owners have their animals perform all manner of dumb antics. Unfortunately, investors often act very much like the owners and pets on the TV show—and it isn't funny. They're overconfident, get trampled by the herd, harbor illusions of control, and refuse to recognize their investment mistakes. The pets actually look smart in comparison.

In recent years, psychologists have studied the aspects of human behavior that influence financial decisions. My Princeton colleague Daniel Kahneman won the Nobel Prize in 2002 for seminal work that spawned the new field of "behavioral finance." Essentially what he and other psychologists tell us is that in investing, we are often our worst enemy. As Pogo used to put it, "We have met the enemy and it is us." An understanding of how vulnerable we are to our own psychology can help us avoid the stupid investor delusions that can screw up our financial security. This final rule points out the major behavioral biases that you must recognize if you are to avoid common investing mistakes. There is an old adage about the game of poker: If you sit down at the table and can't figure out who the sucker is, get up and leave, because it's you. These insights about investor psychology can keep you from being the patsy.

Overconfidence

When psychologists ask a large group of students whether each thinks that he or she is a better driver than the others in the class, 90 percent generally say that they are more skillful drivers. So it is for individual investors who are characteristically overconfident of their ability to select the best stocks or mutual funds in which to invest. These people all too often confuse luck with skill. Again, it's the Lake Wobegon effect, where all the children are above average. Investors, particularly professionals, are convinced that they are endowed with better information and greater skill than others. Professional investors will tell you that that they can pick individual stocks that will beat the market, and most of them truly believe it. But it is impossible for all investors to be above average. Large management fees and large transactions costs that result from excessive trading wipe out any above-average gains. Indeed, because of such fees and costs, most investors actually achieve performance that is distinctly below average.

Charles Ellis, the longtime observer of stock markets and

author of the brilliant investing book *Winning the Loser's Game,* observes that, in the game of amateur tennis, most points are won not by adroit plays on your part but rather by mistakes on the part of your opponent. So it is in investing. Ellis argues that most investors beat themselves by engaging in mistaken stock-market strategies rather than accepting the passive buy-and-hold indexing approach recommended in this book. The way most investors behave, the stock market becomes a loser's game.

How easy it was in early 2000, when the tech stock you bought moved persistently higher, to convince yourself that you were an investment genius. How easy it was then to convince yourself that chasing the last period's best performing mutual fund was a sure strategy for success. And for the few who gave up their day jobs during the bubble to engage in day trading, how exhilarating it was to buy a stock at 10:00 A.M. and find that it had risen 10 percent by noon. All of these strategies ended in disaster. Frequent traders invariably earn lower returns than steady buy-and-hold investors. Terrance Odean, one of the leading researchers in behavioral finance, recommends that if you are thinking of trading (and you are married), consult your wife. The reason is that psychologists have found that women tend to be less overconfident than men.

The first step in dealing with the pernicious effects of overconfidence is to recognize it. Remember Rule 8—Bow to the Wisdom of the Market. Just as the tennis amateur who simply tries to return the ball with no fancy moves is the one who usually wins, so does the investor who simply buys and holds a diversified portfolio comprising all of the stocks that trade in the market.

HERDING

People often feel safety in numbers. It's hard not to get swept up in euphoria during a speculative bubble when all your friends are boasting about their stock-market profits. History is littered with irrational speculative bubbles from Dutch tulip bulbs to U.S. Internet stocks. And it's reassuring to own the mutual funds that are receiving accolades in the press. After all, it would appear to be a sign of wisdom to own the fund that everyone knows was among the best during recent periods.

Unfortunately, in the stock market, past is not prologue. Purchasing the best-performing stocks or funds invariably reflects conventional wisdom, but that wisdom is usually wrong. Indeed, it is often the case that the worst performing funds in the past are the funds that produce the better future returns. People are subject to the fallacy of the hot streak in examining stock market prices or mutual fund returns. The patterns that we often see in the stock market are not patterns at all. Streaks occur randomly with much greater frequency than people realize. Kahneman and his colleague, the late Amos Tversky, found that people get fooled by randomness in many different contexts, including sporting events.

In describing an outstanding performance by a basketball player, reporters and spectators alike commonly use expressions such as "Alan Iverson has the hot hand" or "Jason Kidd is a streak shooter." Those who play, coach, or otherwise follow basketball are almost universally convinced that if a player has successfully made his last shot, or last few shots, he is more likely to make his next shot. In fact, the "hot hand" phenomenon is a myth.

Kahneman and Tversky did a detailed study of every shot taken by the Philadelphia 76ers over a full season and a half. They found no evidence of any positive correlation between the outcomes of successive shots. Indeed, they found that a hit by a player followed by a miss was actually a bit likelier than the case of making two baskets in a row. When the researchers looked at sequences of more than two shots, they found that the number of long streaks (that is, hitting several baskets in a row) was no greater than could have been expected in a random set of data (such as flipping coins in which every event is independent of its predecessor). Although the event of making one's last two or three shots clearly influenced the player's perception of whether he would make his next shot, the hard evidence was that there was no effect. The researchers then confirmed their study by examining the free-throw records of the Boston Celtics and by conducting controlled shooting experiments with the men and women of the Cornell University varsity basketball teams. The outcomes of previous shots influenced players' predictions but not their performance.

These findings do not imply that basketball is a game of chance rather than skill. Obviously there are players who are more adept at making baskets and free throws than others. The point is, however, that the probability of making a shot is independent of the outcome of previous shots. The psychologists conjecture that the persistent belief in the hot hand could be due to memory bias. If long sequences of hits or misses are more memorable than alternating sequences, observers are likely to overestimate the correlation between successive shots. When events sometimes do come in clusters and streaks, people look for explanations and patterns. They refuse to believe that they are random, even though such clusters and streaks do occur frequently in random data such as are derived from the tossing of a coin. So it is with the stock-market and mutual fund returns as well.

Larry Swedroe, in his *Rational Investing in Irrational Times,* provides a wonderful illustration of how hot streaks occur with much greater frequency than people believe.

> Each year a statistics professor begins her class by asking each student to write down the sequential outcome of a series of one hundred imaginary coin tosses. One student, however, is chosen to flip a real coin and chart the outcome. The professor then leaves the room and returns in fifteen minutes with the outcomes waiting for her on her desk. She tells the class that she will identify the one real coin toss out of the thirty submitted with just one guess. With great persistency she amazes the class by getting it correct. How does she perform this seemingly magical act? She knows that the report with the longest consecutive streak of *H* (heads) or *T* (tails) is highly likely to be the result of the real flip. The reason is that, when presented with a question like which of the following sequences is more likely to occur, *HHHHHTTTTT* or *HTHTHTHTHT,* despite the fact that statistics show that both sequences are equally likely to occur, the majority of people select the latter 'more random' outcome. They thus tend to write imaginary sequences that look much more like *HHTTHTHTTT* than *HHHTTTHHHH.*

Aside from the long-term positive direction of the stock market, streaks of excessively high stock returns do not persist—they are typically followed by lower future returns.

Similarly, the laws of financial gravity also operate in reverse. At least for the stock market as a whole, what goes down has come back up. Yet each era's conventional wisdom typically assumes that unusually good markets will get better and unusually bad markets will get worse. Your best strategy is to ignore the conventional wisdom and herd behavior, which is usually wrong, and simply stay the course with your savings and investment program.

Just as herding induces investors to take greater and greater risks during periods of euphoria, so does the same behavior often lead to many investors simultaneously throwing in the towel when pessimism is rampant. The media often encourages such self-destructive behavior by hyping the severity of market declines and blowing the events out of proportion to gain viewers and listeners. Even without excessive media attention, large market movements encourage buy and sell decisions that are based on emotion rather than logic. Stock-market returns show a strong tendency to revert to the mean—and that mean, over the long run, is up.

Any investment that has become a topic of widespread conversation is likely to be especially hazardous to your wealth. It was true of gold in the early 1980s as the price roared above $800 an ounce, Japanese real estate and stocks in the late 1980s as the Nikkei Stock Index climbed close to the 40,000 level, and Internet-related stocks in the late 1990s and early 2000 as the NASDAQ Index crossed the 5,000 level.

All of these investment fashions led to disaster. I realize that it is very difficult to avoid getting swept up in the madness of crowds and the feeling that you have missed out on the opportunities that the "crowd knows" to be a good deal. But probably the most important lesson you can learn about investing is to avoid the temptation to follow the herd.

Illusion of Control

Psychologists have also identified a tendency for individuals to be fooled by an illusion that they have some control over situations where, in fact, none exists. In one study, subjects were seated in front of a computer screen divided in two by a horizontal line, with a ball fluctuating randomly between the two halves. The people were given a device to press to move the ball upward, but they were warned that random shocks would also influence the ball so that they did not have complete control. Subjects were then asked to play a game with the object of keeping the ball in the upper half of the screen as long as possible. In one set of experiments, the device was not even attached, so the players had absolutely no control over the movements of the ball. Nevertheless, when subjects were questioned after a period of playing the game, they were convinced that they had a good deal of control over the movement of the ball. (The only groups that were not deluded by the illusion of control were those who had been clinically diagnosed with depression.)

In another experiment, an office lottery was conducted with two identical sets of baseball cards. One set was placed in a bin from which one card was to be selected by chance. The other set was distributed to the participants. Half the participants were given a choice of which card to take while the other half were simply given a card. Participants were told that the winner would be the person holding the card that matched the one that would be selected by chance from the bin. The individuals were then told that while all the cards had been distributed, a new player wanted to buy a card. Participants were faced with a choice—sell their cards at some negotiated price or hold onto them and hope to win. Obviously, each card has the same probability of winning. Nevertheless, the prices at which players were willing to sell their cards were systematically higher for those who chose their cards than for the group who had simply been given a card. Insights such as this led to the decision to let state lottery buyers pick their own numbers even though luck alone determines lottery winners.

It is this illusion of control that can lead investors to overvalue a losing stock in their portfolio. It also can lead investors to see trends that do not exist or to believe that they can spot a stock price pattern that will predict future prices. In fact, despite considerable efforts to tease some form of predictability out of stock price data, the development of stock prices from period to period is very close to a random walk, where price changes in the future are essentially unrelated to changes in the past. The same holds for various investing "systems," even if they have apparently worked for decades in the past. For example, the "Dogs of the Dow" investing system (the idea that investors should buy the five or ten stocks in the Dow Jones Industrial Average with the highest yields) produced above-average returns for a long period of time, and many investors believe that by following that strategy they can guarantee a superior outcome. But once the strategy was "discovered" and many "Dogs of the Dow" mutual funds came to market and were sold to the public, it failed to work. The dogs no longer hunted.

Investors also tend to believe that events are more predictable after the fact than before. With the benefit of hindsight, we always know the winning play the quarterback should have called. And "hindsight bias" leads us to believe that events that no one foresaw were, in fact, easily predictable in advance. Consider the talking heads on the financial news networks who tell you confidently why the market rose or fell during the previous session and suggest that the move was predictable in advance.

Similarly, investors attribute any success that they have or that some fund manager has in picking stocks to brilliance rather than luck. As Nassim Taleb writes in his *Fooled by Randomness*, "Lucky fools do not bear the slightest suspicion that they . . . have benefited from a disproportionate share of luck." It is this phenomenon that makes people think that there are brilliant portfolio managers or investment gurus who can foretell the future. Such gurus do not exist. The biggest investment mistakes you can make are attempting to time the market or to select your mutual fund on the basis of good recent performance. The fact is that you are much more likely to end up at the top of the distribution of investment returns by simply buying and holding a low-cost index fund than by chasing the hottest asset class or mutual fund of the recent past.

Loss Aversion

Daniel Kahneman is best known for his work with the late Amos Tversky in helping us understand how individuals behave in risky situations. They found that people are far more distressed at the prospect of losses than they are overjoyed by the possibility of gains. Thus, paradoxically, investors might take greater risks to avoid losses than they would to achieve equivalent gains. Moreover, investors are likely to avoid selling stocks that went down in order to avoid the realization of a loss and the necessity of admitting that they made a mistake. On the other hand, investors are generally willing to discard their winners because that enables them to enjoy the success of being correct.

Sometimes, it is sensible to hold onto a stock that has declined during a market meltdown, especially if you have reason to believe the company is still successful. Moreover, you would suffer double the regret if you sold it and the stock subsequently went up. But it makes no sense to hold onto losing stocks such as Enron and WorldCom because of the mistaken belief that if you don't sell, you have not taken a loss. A "paper loss" is just as real as a realized loss. The decision not to sell is exactly the same as the decision to buy the stock at the current price. Moreover, if you own the stock in a taxable account, selling allows you to take a tax loss and the government will help cushion the blow by lowering the amount of your taxes. Selling your winners may only add to your tax burden.

Other Psychological Pitfalls

While we are on the subject of the dumb things people do about their finances, let's tick off some other common investment pitfalls.

- *Susceptibility to Hot Tip Investing*
  We've all heard the stories. Your Uncle Gene knows about a diamond mine in Zaire that's a guaranteed winner. Please remember that a mine is usually a hole in the ground with a liar standing in front of it. Your cousin's sister-in-law Gertrude was told confidentially about an undiscovered little biotech company. "It's a screaming bargain. It's selling at only a dollar a share, and they're ready to announce a cure for cancer. Think, for $2,000 you can buy 2,000 shares." Tips come at you from all fronts—friends, relatives, the telephone, even the Internet. Don't go there. Steer clear of any hot tips. They are overwhelmingly likely to be the poorest investments of your life. And remember: Never buy anything from someone who is out of breath.

- *Gin Rummy Behavior*
  Many investors move from stock to stock or from mutual fund to fund as if they were selecting and discarding cards in a game of gin rummy. You will accomplish nothing by this behavior except running up commission costs and other trading expenses. In fact, you shouldn't be fretting about individual investments at all. If you buy and hold a broad-based index fund, you will automatically own a position in every promising stock investment that exists. Remember Warren Buffett's investment maxims: Lethargy bordering on sloth remains the cornerstone of our investment style. The correct holding period for the stock market is forever.

- *Believing in Foolproof Schemes*
  You will be told by both amateurs and professionals that schemes exist to pick the best fund managers

and to keep you out of the market when prices are falling. The sad fact is that it can't be done. Sure, there are portfolio strategies that in hindsight produced above-average returns, but they all self-destruct over time. There are even market timing strategies that have been successful for years and even decades. But in the long run market timing can only be accomplished by liars. And as Jack Bogle, a legend of the late twentieth century, has remarked: "After nearly fifty years in this business, I do not know of anybody who has done it [market timing] successfully and consistently. I don't even know anybody who *knows* anybody who has done it successfully and consistently. Yet market timing appears to be increasingly embraced by mutual fund investors and the professional managers of fund portfolios alike."

Ignoring Costs

There is only one aspect of predicting future financial returns that consistently matters. The higher the costs you pay, the poorer your financial results will be. Buy only no-load low-cost mutual funds. If you do buy individual stocks, use a discount broker. Shop around for the best and most cost-effective financial products, including insurance, mortgages, and short-term parking places for cash. And by all means extricate yourself from the credit card death spiral. There is no way you will ever make progress on the road to financial success if you pay credit card interest charges that can run as high as 25 percent. So let's remember cardinal Rule 7—Pay Yourself, Not the Piper—as well as Rule 7A: Never Forget Rule 7.

Getting Entranced by New Issues

Do you think you can make real money by getting in on the ground floor of the initial public offering (IPO) of a new company just coming to market? Particularly during the great Internet bubble that collapsed in 2000, it seemed that IPOs were the sure path to riches. Some successful IPOs began trading at two, three, and (in one case) even seven times the price at which they were first offered to the public. No wonder some investors came to believe that getting in on an IPO was the easiest way to coin money in the stock market.

My advice is that you should not buy IPOs at their initial offering price and that you should *never* buy an IPO just after it begins trading at prices that are generally higher than the IPO price. Historically, IPOs have been a bad deal. In measuring all IPOs five years after their initial issuance, researchers have found that IPOs underperform the total stock market by about 4 percentage points per year. The poor performance starts about six months after the issue is sold. Six months is generally set as the "lockup" period, where insiders are prohibited from selling stock to the public. Once that constraint is lifted, the price of the stock usually tanks.

The investment results are even poorer for individual investors. You will never be allowed to buy the really good IPOs at the initial offering price. The hot IPOs are snapped up by the big institutional investors or the very best wealthy clients of the underwriting firm. If your broker calls to say that IPO shares will be available for you, you can bet that the new issue is a dog. Only if the brokerage firm is unable to sell the shares to the big institutions and the best individual clients will you be offered the chance to buy at the initial offering price. Hence, it will systematically turn out that you will be buying only the poorest of the new issues. There is no money-losing strategy I am aware of that is more likely to be hazardous to your wealth, except perhaps the horse races or the gaming tables of Las Vegas.

Part Three

TAKING STOCK: AN INVESTMENT SCORECARD

The bottom line for this book—or any other financial advice—is: Does it work? Many professionals consider my indexing advice unconventional to say the least—probably because it is so unprofitable for them. But the answer is: This advice does work! These final pages will provide some confidence that you will be embarking on a very successful walk toward achieving your financial goals.

The advice presented here is the same as that recommended for years in all eight editions of my longer book, *A Random Walk Down Wall Street.* While scorecards cannot foretell the future, they do give an accurate picture of how that advice has worked in the past.

The returns from index funds have been generous over the past twenty years. Even more important, perhaps, is that the diversification that I have recommended has served to smooth out the overall performance from quarter to quarter. In many periods when common stocks went down, real estate and bond index funds did well—cushioning and often offsetting the decline. Risk was not eliminated completely, but the road was reasonably smooth—especially for older investors whose portfolios were positioned to be relatively safe.

In the following charts—the Malkiel Investment Scorecard—I show the results that would have been achieved over a twenty-year period for investors in different age brackets and for whom different asset allocations were suggested. I also show, as a measure of risk, the lowest return realized over any quarter during this period, as well as the number of quarters during which the investor would have suffered a loss.

Scorecard No. 1
Returns by Different Asset Allocations
January 1983 through December 2002
*(Numbers in boxes show growth of initial investment of $1,000 by December 2002)**

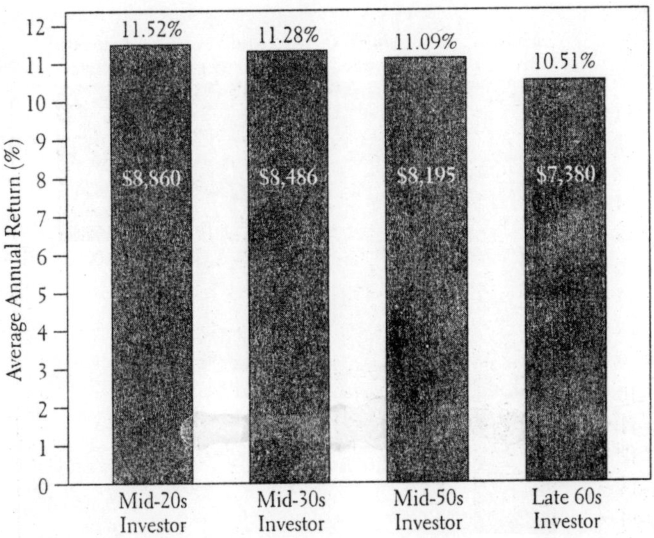

*Assumes dividends and interest reinvested

Scorecard No. 1 shows that the past twenty years have been good ones on average for investors, all of the portfolios recommended in Rule 9 did well. As expected, the investor with the riskiest asset allocation (the investor in her twenties) enjoyed the highest average annual return (11.52%) and the largest final value for her $1,000 initial investment ($8,860). (Remember Basic Point 3—investors who assume more risk will be rewarded with higher returns.) Experience over the past twenty years strongly supports the rules I have suggested for financial success.

SCORECARD NO. 2
RISK ASSUMED BY DIFFERENT ASSET ALLOCATIONS
WORST QUARTERLY RETURN *(January 1983 through December 2002)**
(Numbers in boxes show the number of quarters during which losses were suffered)

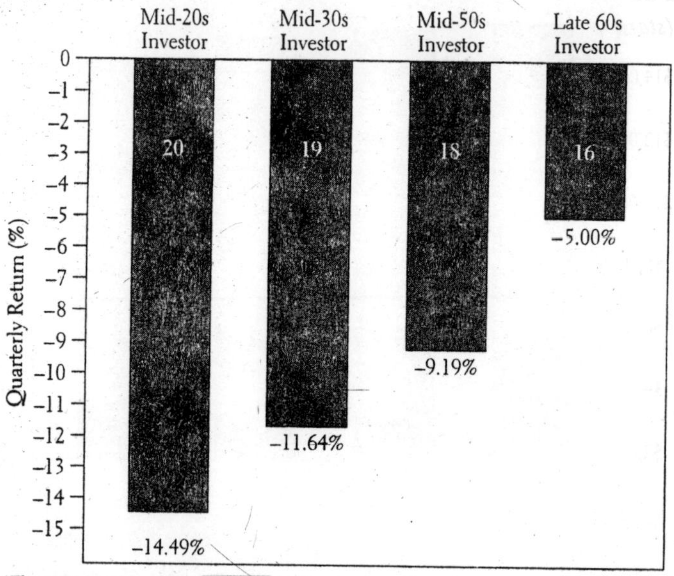

*The worst quarter by return occurred during the October to December quarter of 1987

Scorecard No. 2 makes clear, however, that the different recommended portfolios involved very different risk levels. As an indicator of risk, I show the biggest quarterly loss suffered by investors in different age brackets as well as the number of quarters during which losses were suffered. We see that the twenty-year old investor needed a strong stomach to obtain the extra reward she earned. During the quarter of the October 1987 crash, her portfolio lost almost 15 percent of its value. The biggest quarterly loss was only 5 percent for investors in their late sixties, who had the safest asset allocation. The price paid for extra reward is the acceptance of greater risk.

SCORECARD NO. 3
PORTFOLIO VALUE
(starting value $1,000 on 1/1/83)

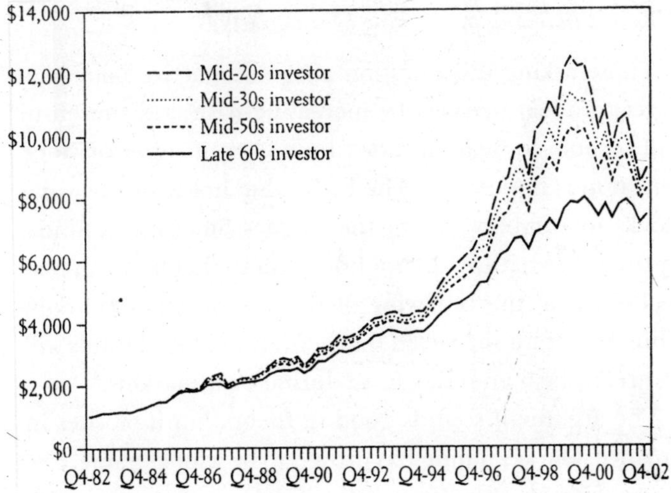

Scorecard No. 3 presents the results during each of the twenty years. The various investors start with $1,000 and we can follow their progress each quarter through the end of 2002. We see again that the mid-20s investor ends up with the most money. The late 60s investor has about $1,500 less but has a much smoother ride, particularly during the early 2000s. Again, we see there is no free lunch in investing. Higher rewards are associated with higher risks.

Questions Frequently Asked About Indexing

As I travel around and talk with investors, certain questions and potential criticisms invariably come up. My indexing investment solution is so easy and profitable that many believe it is simply too good to be true. Here are some questions raised by doubters, and my responses.

"Doesn't indexing fail during bear markets?"

Those asking this question allege that active managers react to down markets by increasing cash and therefore will be able to beat an index fund even if superior stock selection is impossible. The cash value holds steady while stocks are tumbling, so the theory goes. Stock index funds, by their very nature, do not hold cash so that they can perfectly mimic the behavior of the overall stock market. Thus, it is often suggested that actively managed funds will invariably beat an index fund during bear markets.

The argument sounds good in theory but it crashes in practice. Market timing has proved to be a fool's game. I've never known anyone—professional or amateur—who could consistently do it. I've asked my students—brilliant number crunchers—to look at the records of professionally managed mutual funds to see if the fund managers were able to alter their cash positions so as to cushion market declines. They found that when professional fund managers altered their cash positions at different times, they actually made their results even worse. Fund managers tended to hold the least cash just as markets were at their peak, so that they obtained little benefit when the stock market declined. They tended to hold relatively large cash positions at the bottom of bear markets so that they failed to participate fully in the later recovery. Active managers do indeed alter their cash positions, but such changes actually detract from their performance rather than enhancing it. Index funds tend to outperform managed funds in both bull and bear markets. The lesson, and the answer to the question: Whatever the market climate, you will do better with low-expense index funds than with high-expense managed funds.

"Well then, wouldn't an investor have lost almost half her money following your advice during the punishing markets of the early millennium?"

I can hear the chorus of complaints that my scorecards stacked the deck. I have shown you very generous long-run return figures, but most of the last twenty years have been very favorable for investors. So let's examine the most difficult recent period in our securities markets, the first three years of the 2000s, when the stock market experienced unrelenting decline after yearly decline. We all know that this was a terrible period for investors, who suffered through one of the most punishing bear markets in history. And let's examine one of the worst-case scenarios: how would a thirty-something-year-old—investing most of her funds in equities—have fared over the 2000–02 period following my advice? This bear market of the early millennium rivaled the worst periods in stock market history. Would an investor in her thirties with a relatively risky asset allocation have been devastated by following my advice?

Fortunately, the answer is a resounding no. Remember that I have recommended that all investors need to be diversified over different asset classes as well as diversified over time. What that means is that even investors in their thirties need to hold cash, stocks, bonds, and real estate. It also means that investors should avail themselves of the technique of dollar-cost averaging—that is, putting their money into investments gradually over time as would be the case for an investor saving through an IRA or a retirement plan offered by their employer.

As you would expect, younger investors beginning to use my strategy at the top of the market in early 2000 would not have earned positive returns over the three-year period ending in December 2002. But even those heavily invested in equities (which fell by 40 percent) were cushioned by diversification in bonds and real estate that produced positive returns. Moreover, the dollar-cost averaging technique helped reduce risk even further. An investor in her thirties who put $750 per quarter into the various asset categories I recommended would have invested $3,000 per year (the 2002 IRA maximum) or $9,000 total. On December 31, 2002, her investments would have been worth $8,474. Thus, even during one of the most unfavorable periods of market history, the risk-reducing investment techniques I have suggested limited her losses to 5.8 percent of her investment. And if history is any guide, that investor as she approaches her retirement years will, I am convinced, be very happy that she continued to buy equities even as they seemed to be ever falling. Retirees years after the decade of the 1930s were very happy that they stayed the course and continued to pour whatever funds they had at least partially into equities. And current retirees are far better off today if they continued to buy some equities during the very poor stock markets of the 1970s. Investing is a marathon—not a sprint. The prize goes to those with fortitude and endurance.

And what can we say about the investor in his late sixties who is no longer adding to his savings for retirement but rather is ready to begin withdrawing monies? How would that investor have fared following my advice during the severe bear market of the early 2000s? Again, the answer is comforting. I have recommended that investors in their late sixties allocate only 25 percent of their investment funds to equities. Thus, those investors would have been protected by having three quarters of their funds invested in cash, bonds, and real estate—all of which produced positive returns during the early 2000s. In fact, every $100 of that investor's funds that were allocated as I have suggested on January 1, 2000, was worth $116 on December 31, 2002 (a 5 percent annual gain), despite the 40 percent drop in the stock market. While that meager return was nothing to write home about, the late sixties investor was able to earn a return and protect his wealth with the risk-reducing asset allocations I have recommended.

"What would happen if everybody indexed?"

A good question; one that I often hear, when speaking to professional investors. After all, the intellectual case for indexing rests in part on the existence of efficient markets. The reason that stock prices reflect whatever important information is available is that professionals are ready to buy or sell whenever deviations from fair value appear to exist. If the pros did nothing but index, who would do the buying and selling to ensure that market prices reflected new information without delay?

If no professionals were actively seeking out those stocks that had failed to adjust to current economic conditions, I would begin to worry about an indexing strategy. Indexing has become increasingly popular over time, but the proportion of mutual and pension fund assets that are indexed is still barely 10 percent of the total market valuation. As of mid-2003, 90 percent of investment funds are actively managed. When index funds represent 90 percent of the total, I will start to worry. But I suspect that will never happen. Just as kids need to believe in Santa Claus, the hope that one can achieve superior performance will never die. And profit-hungry professional investment managers, who can charge much more for active management, will ensure that the dream of extraordinary returns is kept alive to snare less well informed investors.

"Indexing might be okay for the major frequently traded large U.S. companies, but doesn't the strategy fail in the less efficient markets for foreign and small capitalization stocks?"

Even supporters of an indexing approach often suggest that its applicability should be limited to the large capitalization equities that make up the major stock index in the United States. It is claimed that indexing does not work well for small stocks and for many international markets—especially those in the emerging markets of the world. Here it is suggested that markets are far less efficient and individual stock picking is required for investment success.

In fact, indexing has an enviable record in all markets. Index funds regularly outperform actively managed funds investing in small-cap stocks and foreign equities. Indeed, in these markets where trading is less efficient and more costly, indexing is particularly advantageous. When transactions costs tend to be quite large, a passive buy and hold approach involves substantial cost savings. For example, in many of the small emerging markets of the world, trading costs are particularly large and a variety of exchange taxes make transactions extremely expensive. Thus, the passive indexing approach tends to work especially well in the less efficiently traded markets of the world.

A Summing Up

The message of this book is that over time you will beat the results from most professionally managed accounts by putting regular savings into an investment program using index funds. You also need to diversify your assets over different investment categories according to your age and risk tolerance. These two simple steps are all you need to follow the program. You will achieve wide diversification and incur a minimum of costs. You can cancel your subscriptions to investment services and magazines, and you can disregard all the advice you hear from the media, 99 percent of which is utterly worthless.

You will beat the performance of financial professionals because you now know that expertise in picking individual stocks does not exist. Stock prices too quickly reflect what is known about individual companies to allow anyone to be smarter than the market. No one can honestly claim that they can consistently outperform the market year after year. I've presented extensive evidence that there is lots of randomness in the investing world. Good mutual fund managers in one period of time are scapegoats in the next. Investment strategies that produce above average returns in some years can fail miserably in others. Keep firmly in mind the words that appear in every mutual fund prospectus: **Past results are no guarantee of future performance.** In fact, the reverse is more likely to be true. There are powerful tendencies in any financial market for investment results to revert to the mean. Today's hot stock, today's most successful investment class, today's best mutual fund is very often tomorrow's investment disaster.

The approach may seem dull, dull as dishwater. But hey—it works. The best chance you have to minimize risk and achieve long-run investment success is, first, to diversify among a number of investment categories, including cash, bonds, real estate, and stocks. Then, within each investment category, you will achieve the most effective diversification by purchasing a broad-based index fund that simply buys and holds all the securities comprising that investment category. If you utilize an indexing approach, you will never do worse than the market. No other strategy can make that claim. Even better, chances are that your returns will be higher than those touted by professional managers because the indexing approach guarantees that you will minimize investment costs and fees.

And now, I have a confession to make. After finishing this guide, I have come across another recently published book that has recommended a number of the rules I have suggested here. Scott Adams, the creator of the popular *Dilbert* comic strip, has presented similar rules even more succinctly in his book *Dilbert and the Way of the Weasel.** He boils much of my investment advice into a one-page guide, which is reproduced below:

- Make a **will**.
- Pay off your **credit cards**.
- Get **term life insurance** if you have a family to support.
- Fund your **401k** to the maximum.

* "Everything You Need to Know About Personal Investing" from *Dilbert and the Way of the Weasel* by Scott Adams. Copyright © 2002 by United Media, Inc. Reprinted by permission of HarperCollins Publishers, Inc.

- Fund your **IRA** to the maximum.
- Buy a **house** if you want to live in a house and you can afford it.
- Put six months' **expenses** in a money market account.
- Take whatever money is left over and invest 70 percent in a **stock index fund** and 30 percent in a **bond fund** through any discount broker and never touch it until retirement.
- If any of this confuses you, or if you have something special going on (retirement, college planning, tax issues), hire a **fee-based** financial planner.

I think we have improved on Dilbert's advice, but for starters you could do a lot worse than following Scott Adams's rules.

I have not mentioned making a will, but I certainly agree that everyone should have one. If you have any assets at all, a will can simplify the winding up of your affairs. Moreover, a will can often avoid a very costly probate process.

It's what's *not* covered in Adams's guide that makes every penny you have spent on this book a worthwhile investment. Dilbert's 70–30 rule for the proportion of stocks and bonds is just too general. The asset mix best for you should be tailored to your age, your other sources of income, and especially to your temperament (Rule 5). In Rule 9, I have presented some suggested asset allocation proportions including not only stocks and bonds but also cash and real estate.

And while Dilbert is absolutely correct that index funds are the proper investment vehicle (Rule 8), he doesn't give you Rule 9's list of the best available funds from which to choose, together with the 800 telephone numbers and Web sites. Avoiding the credit card death spiral and buying term insurance is exactly my advice in Rule 7. Costs matter and matter a great deal. Funding your retirement plans to the maximum is exactly what I have recommended in rules 2 and 4.

But where my book really shines is that it shows you how to avoid Dilbert's last rule so that you can fire your expensive financial adviser. Adhering to my ten rules is the only financial advice you need.

DILBERT® by Scott Adams. Reprinted by permission of United Feature Syndicate.

You have a wonderful opportunity to be able to choose early retirement if you start now (Rule 1). Even if you can start by investing as little as $10 or $20 a week, you can build up a substantial nest egg over time. The power of compound interest is one of the strongest forces in the world. You know how to minimize risk (Rule 6) and how to stiff the tax collector (Rule 3). And you've learned how to avoid the most common mistakes made by individuals in arranging their financial affairs (Rule 10). In fact, right now you are probably the smartest investor in your community.

While the securities markets may behave like a random walk, the advice here is one of simple but deliberate steps. It will start you on a walk whose destination is financial fitness and a retirement free of money worries. Happy walking.

REFERENCES

I have suppressed my proclivity for including footnotes with specific references for the books and articles mentioned in the text. Here I list some of the most important works that have informed this investment guide.

Adams, Scott. *Dilbert and the Way of the Weasel.* New York: HarperBusiness, 2002.

Belsky, Gary, and Thomas Gilovich. *Why Smart People Make Big Money Mistakes—And How to Correct Them: Lessons from the New Science of Behavioral Economics.* New York: Fireside, 2000.

William J. Bernstein. *The Intelligent Asset Allocator—How to Build Your Portfolio to Maximize Returns and Minimize Risk.* New York: McGraw-Hill, 2000.

———. *The Four Pillars of Investing: Lessons for Building a Winning Portfolio.* New York: McGraw-Hill, 2002.

Bogle, John C. *Bogle on Mutual Funds: New Perspectives for the Intelligent Investor.* New York: McGraw-Hill, 1994.

———. *Common Sense on Mutual Funds: New Imperatives for the Intelligent Investor.* New York: John Wiley & Sons, 1999.

Brennan, Jack. *Straight Talk on Investing: What You Need to Know.* New York: John Wiley & Sons, 2002.

Cunningham, Lawrence, ed. *The Essays of Warren Buffett: Lessons for Corporate America.* New York: Lawrence Cunningham Publisher, 2001.

Ellis, Charles D. *Winning the Loser's Game.* 4th ed., New York: McGraw-Hill, 2002.

Gardner, David, and Tom Gardner. *The Motley Fool Investment Guide.* New York: Simon & Schuster, 2001.

Kahneman, Daniel, and Mark W. Riepe. "Aspects of Investor Psychology," *Journal of Portfolio Management,* vol. 24, no. 4 (Summer 1998), pp. 52–65.

Kahneman, Daniel, and Amos Tversky. "Prospect Theory: An Analysis of Decision Under Risk," *Econometrica,* vol. 47, no. 2 (1979), pp. 263–91.

LeBaron, Dean, Romesh Vaitilingam, and Marilyn Pitchford. *Dean LeBaron's Book of Investment Quotations.* New York: John Wiley & Sons, 2002.

MacKay, Charles, and Bernard M. Baruch. *Extraordinary Popular Delusions and the Madness of Crowds.* New York: Farrar, Straus & Giroux, 1932.

Odean, Terrance. "Do Investors Trade Too Much?" *American Economic Review,* vol. 89, no. 5 (December 1999), pp. 1279–98.

Quinn, Jane Bryant. *Making the Most of Your Money.* New York: Simon & Schuster, 1997.

Shiller, Robert J. *Irrational Exuberance.* Princeton: Princeton University Press, 2000.

Siegel, Jeremy, and Peter L. Bernstein. *Stocks for the Long Run.* 2nd ed., New York: McGraw-Hill, 1998

Stanley, Thomas J., and William D. Danko. *The Millionaire Next Door: The Surprising Secrets of America's Wealthy.* New York: Pocket Books, 1998.

Swedroe, Larry E. *Rational Investing in Irrational Times: How to Avoid the Costly Mistakes Even Smart People Make Today.* New York: Truman Talley Books, 2002.

Taleb, Nassim Nicholas. *Fooled by Randomness: The Hidden Role of Chance in the Markets and in Life.* New York: Texere, 2001.

Tyson, Eric. *Investing for Dummies.* 3rd ed., New York: John Wiley & Sons, 2003.

INDEX

accounting, fraudulent, 99–100
Adams, Scott, 49, 182–84
Allen, Woody, 6
allocation of assets, 74, 83–95, 172, 183
  life-cycle guide to, 146–52, 173–75, 177–79
  Malkiel Investment Scorecard of, 171–75, 77–78
  overall rate of return determined by, 83
  rebalancing in, 94–95
  risk capacity (financial circumstances) in, 84, 90–92
  risk/return relationship and, 84–87
  temperament (risk tolerance) and, 84, 90, 92–94, 152, 181, 183
  time horizon in, 83–84, 87–90
Amazon.com, 22
apartment house REITs, 25
asset classes, 11–26, 83
  see also bonds; cash; common stocks; real estate
auto insurance, 64

bank certificates of deposit, *see* certificates of deposit (CDs)
bank savings accounts, 12, 59, 61, 62
banks, Internet, 61
Barclay Global Investors, 140
Barron's, 23
Baruch, Bernard, 122
basketball players, 156–58
Beardstown Ladies, 9
bear markets, 28–29, 86–87, 109
  index funds in, 176–79

bear markets (*continued*)
October 1987, 87, 174–75
behavioral finance, 153–67, 184
belief in foolproof schemes in, 164–65
gin rummy behavior in, 164
herd mentality in, 18, 156–60
and ignoring costs, 165–66
illusion of control in, 160–62
IPOs and, 166–67
loss aversion in, 162–63
overconfidence in, 154–55
susceptibility to hot tip investing in, 164
Benartzi, Shlomo, 44–45
Berkshire Hathaway, 133
Berra, Yogi, 83
Best, A. M., insurance company ratings of, 66–67
Bezos, Jeff, 22
Blodgett, Henry, 23
Bogle, Jack, 113, 114, 119, 165
bond index funds, 115, 138, 139, 141, 146, 183, 172
selected, data on, 147
bonds, 11, 13–15, 74–75, 83, 114–15, 183
common stocks vs., 16
coupon payments of, 13–14
in diversification, 96, 97–98, 104–5, 177–78, 179, 182
effective yield of, 14
as fixed-income investments, 14
high- vs. low-quality, 15
inflation rates and, 14, 26, 31
interest rates and, 14, 15, 31, 97
maturity of, 13, 14
returns of, 13–14, 16, 30, 85, 88
risk/return relationship of, 15, 28, 30, 31, 85, 86
safety of, 14–15
tax-exempt, 76, 151–52
total return index of, 38
types of, 13, 14–15; *see also* corporate bonds; municipal bonds; Treasury bonds
volatility of, 85, 86
see also allocation of assets
Boomer generation, 50, 56, 72
Boston, Mass., Ben Franklin's gift to, 39–40
Boston Celtics, 157
Brennan, Jack, 50, 55–56
brokerage commissions, 114, 116, 117, 127, 140, 164
brokers, 57–58
discount, 116, 140, 165, 183
bubbles, 18–24
Internet, 21–23, 50, 122, 155, 159, 166
Japanese real estate, 26, 159
South Sea, 20–21
tulip-bulb, 19–20
budgets, 45–46, 54
Buffett, Warren, 108–9, 131, 133, 134, 138, 164
Bush, George W., 77

capital gains, 28, 84
car insurance, 64
car loans, 49, 52
cars, 47, 54
cash, 11, 12–13, 83, 165, 183
average annual return of, 85
definition of, 12
diversification and, 96, 97, 177–78, 179, 182
inflation rates and, 30–31
life insurance and, 64–65

mutual funds and, 122, 176–77
risk/return relationship of, 28, 30–31, 84, 85, 86
see also allocation of assets
cash flow, 52
cash reserve, 13, 57–63
CDs in, 58, 60–61, 62
establishment of, 57–58
Internet banks for, 61
money-market funds in, 58–59, 62
tax-exempt money market funds in, 62–63
Treasury bills in, 61–62
certificates of deposit (CDs), 12, 59, 84
in cash reserve, 58, 60–61, 62
disadvantages of, 60
FDIC insured, 60, 61, 97
interest of, 60–61
Cervantes, Miguel de, 96
chance, laws of, 131–33, 137
herd mentality and, 156–60
checking accounts, 12
interest-bearing, 13
check-writing privileges, 13, 58, 61, 62
Cisco, 139
Clements, Jonathan, 48–49, 131
CNBC, 8, 98
Cohen & Steers Realty, 148
collectibles, 11–12
college tuitions, 15, 58, 60, 88
determining financial aid for, 80
commercial paper (short-term corporate IOUs), 59
commercial real estate, 25
commissions, 65, 66, 67
brokerage, 114, 116, 117, 127, 140, 164
of investment advisers, 6–7, 8
common stocks, 11, 15–24, 74–75, 76, 141, 172, 176
bonds vs., 16
capital gains of, 28, 84
discount brokers for direct purchase of, 116, 140, 165, 183
in diversification, 16, 24, 96, 98–105, 177–78, 182
dividends of, 16, 27, 28, 89
dollar-cost averaging and, 106–10
as equity securities, 16; *see also* equity funds
estimated future growth of, 17–18
high-tech, 86, 96, 122, 140, 155
inflation rates and, 31
international, 103–4, 105
investment period and, 87–89
IPOs of, 7, 22–23, 166
large capitalization, 138, 143–44, 180
as ownership interest, 15–16
price bubbles in, *see* bubbles
price-earnings (P/E) ratio of, 17–18
REITs vs., 26
returns of, 16, 26, 28, 84–85, 87–88, 143–44
risk/return relationship of, 16, 28–29, 30, 31, 84–87
small capitalization, 138, 143–44, 180–81
total market capitalization of, 22
total market value of, 144
total return index of, 38
volatility of, 16–17, 28, 85

common stocks (*continued*)
see also allocation of assets; index funds; mutual funds; stock market
Compaq, 143
compound interest, 37–41, 184
accumulations resulting from, 39–41
process of, 38–39
rule of 72 in, 39
Consumer Price Index (CPI), 38
control, illusion of, 160–62
Cornell University, 157
corporate bonds, 13
risk/return relationship of, 15, 28, 30, 31
yield of, 39
costs, 111–17, 136, 181
credit card balances in, 49–50, 52, 112–13, 165, 182, 183–84
ignoring, in behavioral finance, 165–66
market impact, 127
opportunity, 47–48
of variable annuities, 67, 115
of whole life insurance, 64–65, 115
of wrap accounts, 117
see also commissions; expense ratios; transaction costs
coupon booklets, newspaper, 48
coupon payments, bond, 13–14
credit card balances, 49–50, 52, 112–13, 165, 182, 183–84
cubes (NASDAQ 100), 139–40
currency, 12
dollar, value of, 31, 103
European, value of, 103

Danko, William, 54–55
day trading, 116, 118, 155
dealer spreads, 140, 142
Diamonds, 140
Digiscents, 22
Dilbert and the Way of the Weasel (Adams), 182–84
Dimensional Fund Advisors, 125
disability insurance, 58
discount brokers, 116, 140, 165, 183
discount retailers, 48
diversification, 15, 24, 96–110, 171–72, 181
adequate amount of, 100–102
adversity reduced by, 98, 99
benefits of, 96–98
bonds in, 96, 97–98, 104–5, 177–78, 179, 182
cash and, 96, 97, 177–78, 179, 182
common stocks in, 16, 24, 96, 98–105, 177–78, 182
dollar-cost averaging in, 106–10, 178
of equity funds, 102, 104–5
of 401(k) plans, 99–100
index funds in, 135, 138, 141, 144, 171–72
international stocks in, 103–4, 105
real estate in, 25–26, 96, 98, 104, 105, 141, 177–78, 179, 182
REITs in, 25–26, 105
dividends, 16, 26, 27, 28, 89
reinvested, 240–41
Dixon, Joel, 76
"Dogs of the Dow" investing system, 161–62
dollar, value of, 31, 103

dollar-cost averaging, 106–10, 178
  benefits of, 108
  illustration of, 107
Don Quixote (Cervantes), 96
Doonesbury (Trudeau), 124–25
Dow Jones Industrial Average, 85, 86–87, 93, 142, 161–62
  ETFs of, 140
Dreyfus Bond Market Index Basic Fund, 147

EAFE index, 103, 142
eBay, 17, 140
economic recessions, 104
Education Savings Accounts (ESAs), 80
education savings bonds, government, 81
education savings plans, *see* tax-free education savings plans
efficient-market theory (EMT), 17–18, 23–24, 119–21, 124, 135
Einstein, Albert, 3, 37
electronic trading, 116
Ellis, Charles, 9–10, 122–23, 154–55
England, 19, 20–21
Enron Corporation, 15, 98–99, 143, 163
equity funds, 124–27, 136
  average returns of, 126
  diversification of, 102, 104–5
  expense ratios of, 137–38
  index funds vs., 124–26, 137–38
  large-cap vs. small-cap, 138
equity securities, 16
  see also common stocks
exchange traded funds (ETFs), 139–41
expense ratios, 111–12, 113–15, 154, 177
  of equity funds, 137–38
  of ETFs, 140
  of index funds, 115, 126–27, 135, 136, 144, 146
  of money-market funds, 58, 114–15
Extraordinary Popular Delusions and the Madness of Crowds (MacKay), 19
ezboard.com, 22

Federal Deposit Insurance Corporation (FDIC), 12, 60, 61, 97
fiber-optic networks, 18, 98
Fidelity Group, 79, 133–34
  Magellan Fund, 133–34
  Municipal Money Market Fund, 63
  Real Estate fund, 148
  Spartan Money Market Fund, 59
  Spartan Total Index Fund, 145
Fidelity "Planning Center," 53
financial aid, college, 80
Financial Engines, 53
financial professionals, 6, 118–19, 120, 121, 124–34, 135, 143, 154, 162, 179–80, 181, 183
  individual strategies of, 133–34
  laws of chance and, 131–33, 137
  most shares owned by, 126
  mutual fund managers, 122, 124, 125, 126–34, 164–65, 176–77, 182

financial professionals (*continued*)
  securities analysts, 23, 98
  successful, 127–34
  see also investment advisers
financial publications, 7, 8–9, 26
529 college savings accounts, 78–80, 81
fixed-income investments, 14
Fooled by Randomness (Taleb), 8, 162
foolproof schemes, belief in, 164–65
Forbes, 9, 130, 138
Forbes, Malcolm, 9
Forbes Honor Roll funds, 130
401(k) pension plans, 126, 146, 182
  annual limits for, 73
  employer matching contributions to, 43–44, 73, 75, 99, 100
  invested in own company stock, 99–100
  of over-fifty investors, 51, 73
403(b) pension plans, 51, 73, 75
Franklin, Benjamin, 39–40, 46
fraudulent accounting, 99–100
future expenditures, large, 15, 58, 60
  see also college tuitions

Gabriella, Mark, 49
General Motors, 17
Giangardella, Mike, 49
gin rummy behavior, 164
globalization, 103–4
gold, 11, 12, 159
  total return index of, 38
Goldwyn, Samuel, 17
Google search engine, 61
Government National Mortgage Association (Ginny Mae) bonds, 13
Grady, Todd, 39
Graham, Katharine, 133
Gray, Thomas, 11
Great Depression, 86, 87
growth companies, 17–18, 27, 28, 144
growth indexes, 138, 139
Grubman, Jack, 23

health insurance, 64
herd mentality, 18, 156–60
Hewlett Packard, 143
high-tech stocks, 86, 96, 122, 140, 155
hindsight bias, 162, 165
Holland, 19–20
home equity, 52
home equity loans, 52
  tax-deductible interest of, 112
home insurance, 64
home ownership, 24–25, 183
  as tax strategy, 81–82, 112
  see also mortgages
hotel REITs, 25
"hot" funds, 128–29
hot streaks, fallacy of, 156–59
  memory bias in, 157–58
hot tip investing, 164

IBM, 17
illusion of control, 160–62
incubator funds, 133–34
indexes, 9, 138–39, 142–46
  EAFE, 103, 142
  growth, 138, 139
  Morgan Stanley Capital Emerging Markets, 103, 142

NASDAQ, 86, 159
Nikkei Stock, 159
Russell 3,000, 139, 142
S&P 500, 100, 123, 124–26, 142–44
value, 138, 139
Wilshire 5,000–Total Stock Market, 139, 142, 144
index funds, 115, 120, 121, 131, 134, 135–52, 171–84
advantages of, 136–38
in bear markets, 176–79
bond, 115, 138, 139, 141, 146, 147, 172
buy-and-hold approach to, 115, 155, 162, 164, 180–81, 182
cost-efficiency of, 136
in diversification, 135, 138, 141, 144, 171–72
EAFE, 142
equity funds vs., 124–26, 137–38
exchange traded (ETFs), 139–41
expense ratios of, 115, 126–27, 135, 136, 144, 146
frequently asked questions about, 176–81
growth, 138, 139
indexes tracked by, 138–39, 142–46
international, 141–42, 146, 180–81
no-load, low-expense, 144–45, 146, 147, 148, 183
passively managed, 135–36, 144
performance of, 124–25, 135–36, 141–42, 181–82
as potential universal investment strategy, 179–80
predictability of, 137
professional managers of, 143
reinvested dividends of, 140
REITs, 141, 146, 148
returns of, 123, 126, 137, 171–75, 182
simplified investing in, 136
small capitalization, 180–81
strategy of, 136
tax-efficiency of, 76–77, 137
"Total Stock Market," 139, 140, 142, 144–46
transaction costs of, 140, 143, 180–81
value, 138, 139
Individual Retirement Accounts (IRAs), 40–41, 69–72, 75–76, 140, 178, 182
annual contribution limits for, 71
of over-fifty investors, 51, 71
Roth, 71–72, 77, 78
SEP-, 74
taxable investing vs., 70–71
tax advantages of, 69–71
inflation rates, 14, 105, 149
bonds and, 14, 26, 31
cash and, 30–31
common stocks and, 31
real estate and, 26, 31, 82
total return indices and, 38
inherited wealth, 54
initial public offerings (IPOs), 7
behavioral finance and, 166–67
of Internet bubble, 22–23, 166
insurance, 11, 63–67, 91, 165

insurance (*continued*)
of discount brokerage accounts, 116
FDIC, 12, 60, 61, 97
of municipal bonds, 14–15
see also life insurance
Intel, 139
interest, 13, 30
bonds and, 14, 15, 31, 97
of CDs, 60–61
credit card, 112
on money-market funds, 58, 59, 61
on mortgages, 52, 81, 82
tax-deductible, 81, 112
see also compound interest
Internal Revenue Service, 74, 75
international index funds, 141–42, 146
transaction costs of, 180–81
international stocks, 103–4, 105
Internet, 17–18, 55, 68, 164
discount sales on, 48
Google search engine of, 61
see also Web sites
Internet banks, 61
Internet bubble, 21–23, 50, 122, 155, 159, 166
investing systems, 161–62
investment advisers, 5–10, 89, 138, 183, 184
commissions earned by, 6–7, 8
expertise lacked by, 5, 7–10
overtrading by, 6
investment banking, 23
investment categories, 11–26, 83
see also bonds; cash; common stocks; real estate
investment period, 87–89
Investment Planning and Tools, 53
Irrational Exuberance (Shiller), 18–19

jailhouse REITs, 25
Japan, 103
Japanese real estate bubble, 26, 159
Johnson & Johnson, 17
junk bonds, 15

Kahneman, Daniel, 44, 153, 156–57, 162–63
Keillor, Garrison, 126
Keogh pension plans, 63–74, 75–76
Kindleberger, Charles, 18

large-capitalization stocks, 138, 143–44, 180
La Rochefoucauld, François, 6th Duc de, 55
Lay, Kenneth, 98
Letterman, David, 153
life insurance, 64–67
Best ratings of, 66–67
cash value of, 64–65
life expectancy and, 66
premiums of, 66
sales commissions on, 65, 66, 67
term, *see* term life insurance
variable annuities, 67, 76, 115
Web sites for, 66
whole, 64–65, 115
lifestyle, downsizing of, 51
Lifetime Savings Accounts, 77–78
load charges, 114
Loser's Game, The (Ellis), 9
loss aversion, 44–45

in behavioral finance, 162–63
lotteries, 160–61
Lynch, Peter, 131, 133–34, 138

McGwire, Mark, 64
machine-gun company, 21
MacKay, Charles, 19
Magellan Fund, 133–34
Making the Most of Your Money (Quinn), 6–7
Malkiel Investment Scorecard, 171–75, 177–78
Manhattan Island, purchase of, 40
market impact costs, 127
Massachusetts, 79
media, 7–9, 98, 159, 162, 181
 Internet bubble and, 23
medical insurance, 58
medicine, field of, 9
Meeker, Mary, 23
memory bias, 157–58
Merck, 17
mergers, 143
Microsoft, 17, 100, 139
Millionaire Next Door, The (Stanley and Danko), 54–55
millionaires, 54–56
 of Vanguard Group, 55–56
mines, 164
money-market funds, 12–13, 58–59, 183
 check-writing privileges of, 13, 58, 61, 62
 diversification and, 97
 expense ratios of, 58, 114–15
 interest of, 58, 59, 61
 low-expense, 59, 63
 returns of, 58, 59, 62
 tax-exempt, 62–63
Morgan, J. P., 93, 152
Morgan Stanley Capital International Emerging Markets Index, 103, 142
Morningstar, 138
Morningstar Mutual Fund Service, 115, 130–31, 138
mortgages, 25, 91, 165
 interest on, 52, 81, 82
 paid off, 52
 reverse, 52
Motley Fool Investment Guide, 46
municipal bonds, 13
 insured, 14–15
 safety of, 14
Murphy's Law, 57
mutual funds, 7, 74–75, 78, 117, 156, 162
 brokerage commissions paid by, 114, 127
 cash positions of, 122, 176–77
 dollar-cost averaging and, 106–10
 expense ratios of, 58, 111–12, 113–15, 126–27, 137–38, 177
 "hot," 128–29
 incubator, 133–34
 Internet bubble and, 122
 load charges of, 114
 market impact costs of, 127
 no-load, 140, 165
 number of, 132
 performance of, 124–26, 127, 128–31, 137–38, 181–82
 professional managers of, 122, 124, 125, 126–34, 164–65, 176–77, 182
 REITs and, 25–26
 tax-inefficient, 76–77
 transaction costs of, 113, 115, 127, 136
 variable annuities and, 67, 115

mutual funds (*continued*)
  see also specific fund types

NASDAQ, 139, 144
NASDAQ Index, 86, 159
NASDAQ 100 exchange traded fund, 139–40
New Economy, 22–23, 98, 140
Newton, Isaac, 21
New York State, 79
New York Stock Exchange, 25, 116, 144
Nikkei Stock Index, 159

Odean, Terrance, 155
office building REITs, 25
opportunity costs, 47–48
overconfidence, 154–55
  gender differences in, 155
overtrading, 6
ownership shares, shipping, 97

panics, stock market, 109–10
paper losses, 163
payroll deduction plans, 43–44
Pebble Beach Golf Course, 26
pension plans, 69, 73–75, 126, 144, 178
  403(b), 51, 73, 75
  investment choices for, 74–75
  self-employed, 73–74, 75–76
  see also 401(k) pension plans
Philadelphia, Pa., Ben Franklin's gift to, 39–40
Philadelphia 76ers, 157
Pogo, 153–54
Ponzi scheme, 19
positive feedback loop, 18–19
price-earnings (P/E) ratio, 17–18
Priceline.com, 22
principal, safety of, 12, 13, 59
professionals, financial, *see* financial professionals
property taxes, 81
psychology, investor, *see* behavioral finance
Public Agenda, 42–43

Quinn, Jane Bryant, 6–7
random walk, 121, 130, 161, 184
Random Walk Down Wall Street, A (Malkiel), 146, 171
Rational Investing in Irrational Times (Swedroe), 93, 158
real estate, 11, 24–26, 83, 139, 141, 148, 172, 177–78, 183
  average annual returns of, 85
  commercial, 25
  in diversification, 25–26, 96, 98, 104, 105, 141, 177–78, 179, 182
  individual home ownership as, 24–25, 81–82
  inflation rates and, 26, 31, 82
  in Japanese bubble, 26, 159
  risk/return relationship of, 28, 31
real estate investment trusts (REITs), 25–26, 117
  in diversification, 25–26, 98, 105
  index funds of, 141, 146, 148
  in life-cycle guide to asset allocation, 149–51
  returns of, 26
rebalancing, 94–95
recessions, economic, 104
retailers, discount, 48
retirement, 15, 24, 37, 42–43, 102, 139, 178, 183, 184
  allocation of assets in, 89–90, 95, 149, 151

outliving one's money in, 56, 65
pushing back date of, 51–52
see also savings; tax-advantaged retirement plans
retirement planning, 52–53
Retirement Savings Accounts (RSAs), 77, 78
reverse mortgages, 52
risk, definition of, 84, 85
risk capacity, 84, 90–92
risk/return relationship, 10, 27–32, 173, 174–75
and allocation of assets, 84–87
annual volatility in, 28
of bonds, 15, 28, 30, 31, 85, 86
of cash, 28, 30–31, 84, 85, 86
of common stocks, 16, 28–29, 30, 31, 84–87
of corporate bonds, 15, 28, 30, 31
definition of, 27
of real estate, 28, 31
of Treasury bills, 85, 86
of Treasury bonds, 27, 30, 85, 86
risk tolerance (temperament), 84, 90, 92–94, 152, 181, 183
Rockefeller Center, 26
Roth IRAs, 71–72, 77, 78
rule of 72, 39
Russell 3,000 Index, 139, 142

Salomon Brothers, 133
Save More Tomorrow Plan, 44–45
savings, 37–56, 139, 184
budgeting in, 45–46, 54
cash value of life insurance as, 64–65
changed spending habits in, 46–47
downsizing one's lifestyle in, 51
home equity in, 52
importance of, 42–43
loss aversion and, 44–45
millionaires created by, 54–56
opportunity costs and, 47–48
paid-off credit cards in, 49–50, 52
payroll deduction plans in, 43–44
pushing back retirement date in, 51–52
regular, 42–56
for retirement, *see* tax-advantaged retirement plans
Save More Tomorrow Plan in, 44–45
saving on spending in, 48–49
strategies for catching up on, 50–52, 71, 73
techniques for, 43–50
time as money in, 37–41, 48; *see also* compound interest
savings accounts, bank, 12, 59, 61, 62
Lifetime, 77–78
Retirement, 77, 78
Schwab:
1000 Investor Fund, 145
Total Bond Market Index Fund, 147
Schwed, Fred, Jr., 5
Sector Spyders, 140
securities analysts, 23, 98

Securities and Exchange Commission, 115
securities salesmen, 6–7
Security Investors Protection Corporation, 116
self-employed, pension plans for, 73–74, 75–76
SEP-IRA plan, 74
Sharpe, William, 96–97
Shiller, Robert, 18–19
shipping ownership shares, 96
shopping mall REITs, 25
Shoven, John, 76
Siegel, Jeremy, 38
Sinquefield, Rex, 125
small-capitalization stocks, 138, 143–44, 180–81
Social Security, 51, 52
Soros, George, 16
South Sea Bubble, 20–21
spending:
  changed habits of, 46–47
  saving on, 48–49
Spyders, 140
Standard & Poor's 500–Stock Index (S&P 500), 29, 100, 123, 124–26, 142–44
  changes in composition of, 143
  component stocks' pricing affected by, 143
  ETFs of, 140
  market value represented by, 144
Stanley, Thomas, 54–55
state income tax returns, 79
state lotteries, 161
State Street Investors, 140
state tax-exempt funds, 63
Stern, Howard, 23
St. Louis Cardinals baseball team, 64
stock issues, *see* initial public offerings (IPOs)
stock market, 41, 105, 118–34, 141, 152, 155
  bear, *see* bear markets
  day trading on, 116, 118, 155
  dollar-cost averaging and, 106–10
  in economic recessions, 104
  efficient-market theory of, 17–18, 23–24, 119–21, 124, 135, 179–80
  electronic trading on, 116
  global, 104
  hot streaks in, 156–59
  panics in, 109–10
  paper losses in, 163
  pessimism and, 159
  as random walk, 121, 130, 161, 184
  timing of, 41, 122–24, 162, 165, 176
  unpredictability of, 118–21, 161–62
  upward bias of, 29–30, 120–21, 159
  see also bubbles; financial professionals; indexes
stocks, *see* common stocks
Stocks for the Long Run (Siegel), 38
stock tips, 8, 164
Straight Talk on Investing (Brennan), 50
Student Loan Marketing Association (Sallie Mae) bonds, 13
Swedroe, Larry, 93, 158
systems, investing, 161–62

Taleb, Nassim Nicholas, 8, 162
Talmud, 149

tax-advantaged retirement plans, 43–44, 64, 65, 67, 68–78, 88, 151
- ETFs and, 140
- life insurance in, 64
- Lifetime Savings Accounts, 77–78
- possible new, 77–78
- potential disadvantage of, 77
- priorities in saving for, 75–77
- Retirement Savings Accounts (RSAs), 77, 78
- variable annuities in, 76
- *see also* individual retirement accounts (IRAs); pension plans

tax brackets, 43, 69, 70
tax efficiency:
- of ETFs, 140
- of index funds, 76–77, 137

taxes, 44, 48, 68–82, 121, 184
- buying vs. selling and, 163
- home ownership and, 81–82, 112
- interest deductible from, 81, 112
- property, 81
- state income, 79

tax-exempt securities, 75
- bonds, 76, 151–52
- state, 63
- T-bill income, 62

tax-free education savings plans, 78–81
- Education Savings Accounts (ESAs), 80
- education savings bonds, 81
- 529 college savings accounts, 78–80, 81

temperament (risk tolerance), 84, 90, 92–94, 152, 181, 183

term life insurance, 64, 65–67, 115, 182, 183–84
- decreasing, 65
- level-premium, 66
- renewable, 65, 66

Thaler, Richard, 44–45
TIAA-CREF, 67, 79
- Equity Index Fund, 145
- Money Market Fund, 59
- Real Estate Securities Fund, 148

Time, 22
time horizon, 83–84, 87–90
Tomlin, Lily, 9
"Total International Stock Index Funds," 146
total market capitalization, 22
total market value, 144
total return indices, 38
"Total Stock Market" index funds, 139, 142, 144–46
- ETF, 140
- selected, data on, 145

transaction costs, 113, 115, 121, 127, 136, 142, 154, 182
- of ETFs, 140–41
- of index funds, 140, 143, 180–81
- of international trading, 180–81

Treasury bills (T-bills), 12, 61–62
- average annual return of, 85
- diversification and, 97
- risk/return relationship of, 85, 86

Treasury bonds, 13, 27, 97
- average annual return of, 85
- education savings, 81
- interest and, 31
- risk/return relationship of, 27, 30, 85, 86

Treasury bonds (*continued*)
safety of, 14
total return index of, 38
trophy properties, 26
T. Rowe Price Total Equity Market Index Fund, 145
Trudeau, Garry, 124–25
tulip-bulb bubble, 19–20
Tversky, Amos, 156–57, 162–63

USAA:
Income Fund, 147
Money Market Fund, 59
Tax-Exempt Money Market Fund, 63
VA Linux, 23
value indexes, 138, 139
Value Line, 138
Vanguard Group of Investment Companies, 50, 53, 67, 79, 113, 119
millionaire investors of, 55–56
Money Market (prime portfolio), 59
REIT Index Fund, 148
Tax-Exempt Money Market Fund, 63
Total Bond Market Index Fund, 147
Total Stock Market Index Fund, 145
variable annuities, 67, 76, 115
variable life insurance, 65
Viner, Jack, 35–36
Vipers, 140
volatility, 16–17, 26, 28, 85, 86, 105

Wall Street Journal, 48–49, 131
warehouse REITs, 25
Washington, George, 39
Washington Post Company, 133
Web sites, 22
bond index funds, 147
CD rates, 60–61
expense ratios, 115
life insurance, 66
low-expense money-market funds, 59, 63
real estate funds, 148
retirement planning, 52–53
tax-exempt money-market funds, 63
Total Stock Market Index Funds, 145
U.S. Treasury, 62, 81
Weiss Research, 67
Whalen, Charles, 64
whole life insurance, 64–65, 115
wills, 182, 183
Wilshire 5,000–Total Stock Market Index, 139, 142
entire U.S. market represented by, 144
Wilson, Bill, 49
Winning the Loser's Game (Ellis), 155
WorldCom, 15, 97, 99–100, 163
P/E ratio of, 17–18
wrap accounts, 117

zero coupon bonds, 14
Zweig, Jason, 121–22